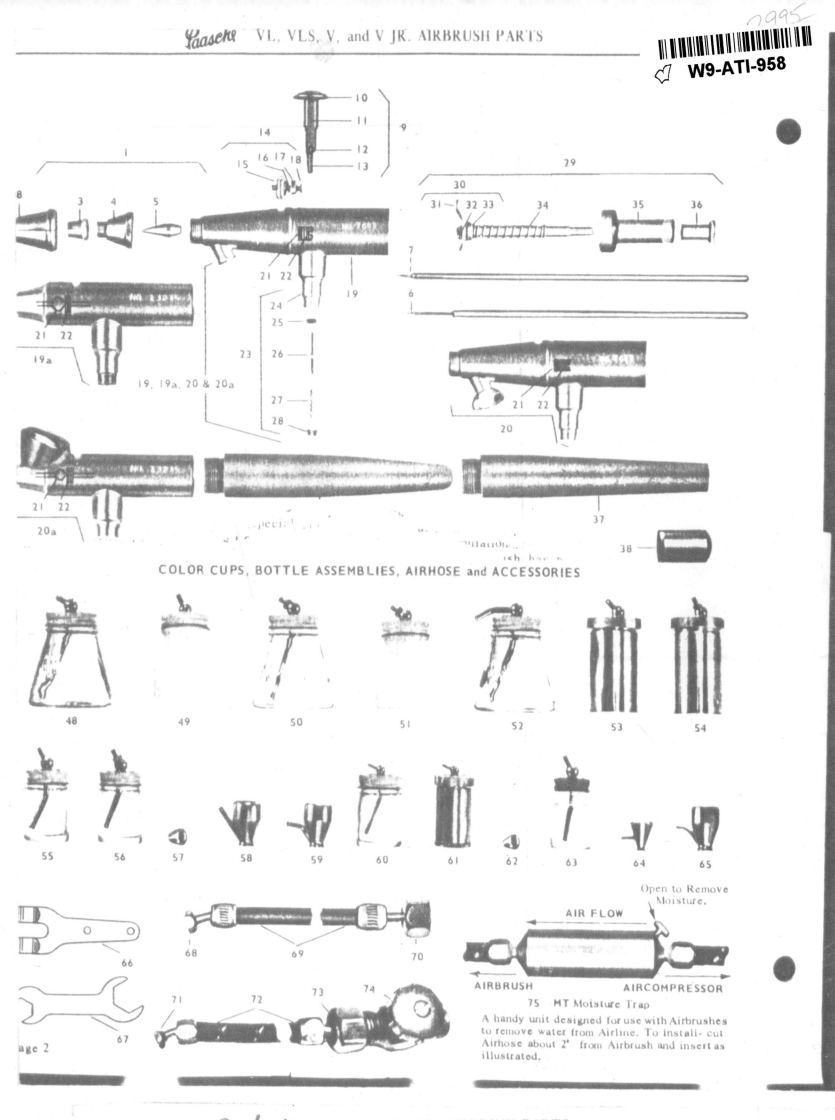

COLOR CUPS, BOTTLE ASSEMBLIES, AIRHOSE and ACCESSORIES

75 MT Moisture Trap

A handy unit designed for use with Airbrushes to remove water from Airline. To install- cut Airhose about 2" from Airbrush and insert as illustrated.

Open to Remove Moisture.

AIR FLOW

AIRBRUSH   AIRCOMPRESSOR

Page 2

Air Powered

Air Powered

The Art of the Airbrush

A
**Richard H. Childers
Production**

Text

Elyce Wakerman

Design

**Bob Zoell
Rick Probst
W. Scott Griffiths**

RANDOM HOUSE

New York

Acknowledgments

We gratefully acknowledge the assistance of the following people and institutions in the preparation of this book.

Vince Arcaro
Anne M. Barrie
Julian Barry
Linda Barton
Lynn Berman
Christine Beauregard
Karl Bornstein
Michael Borders
Mike and Janean Bruston
Barry Burrow
Jill Caldwell
Thomas Childers
Astrid Conti
Doris E. Cook
Jim Cox
Jean & Richard Coyne
Shirley Crane
Denise Dervin
Disney Studios
Katherine M. Dunlop
Barry Friedman
George Garvin
G-2 Graphic Service
Graphic Process
Jules Greenblatt

Judie Gregg
Bill Griffith
Guho's Religious Books
Heidi Handman
Mark Hanks
Joanne Hedge
Debbie Holvick
Donna Huyssen
Joe King
Jay Kinney
Les Landau
Hal Lawrence
Esther Lewis
William H. Lyles
Peter Miller
Mirage Gallery
Murder Incorporated
Ed Newton
Diane Noomin
Art Paul
Jerry & Murray Ross
R S Typographics
Clint Ryno
Ian Sander
Steve Schapiro
Joyce Seifert
Art Spiegelman
Steven Spielberg
Selma Wakerman
Jeff Werner

Marshall Wolff
David Wollenberg
Joyce Zavarro
Laura Ziskin

A special thanks to those who contributed time and material to the project.

Pat Barry & J. B. Wilson
Dave Black
Jim Camperos
Shirley Crane
Terence Flynn
Norm Gollin
Thomas LaFortune
Robert Moses
Paperback Jack
Chris Pearson
Lisa Powers
Pamela Prince
Roger Rebbun
Al Sander
Susan Sexton
Steve Sheppard
Stuart Siegel
UCLA Libraries
Charles White III
Charlie Wild
Glenn Zacher

Grateful acknowledgment is made to the following for permission to reprint previously published material: Excerpt from 'Easter Parade' by Irving Berlin © Copyright 1933 Irving Berlin • © Copyright renewed Irving Berlin • Reprinted by permission of Irving Berlin Music Corporation; Flesh and Fantasy by Penny Stallings © 1978, reprinted by permission of St. Martin's Press, N.Y.
Library of Congress Cataloging in Publication Date • Richard H. Childers Productions • AIRPOWERED • Bibliography: p. • 1. Airbrush art I. Title • NC915.A35R5   741.2'9   79-5083 • ISBN 0-394-50755-X
Manufactured in the United States of America • First Edition

23456789

Credits

Producer
Richard H. Childers

Text
Elyce Wakerman

Design
Bob Zoell
Rick Probst
W. Scott Griffiths

Associate Producer
Stephen Rosenberg

Associate Producer
Aileen Sander Childers

Associate Producer
Gerald Lavelle

Photography
Steve Shaffer

Research
Joel Goldstein

Production
Abigail Yokoshima

Production Assistant
Cher Fenley

Legal Advisor
Hobart Kelliston McDowell, III

The Random House Staff

Art Director
R. D. Scudellari

Publishing Director
Anthony Schulte

Editor
Gary Fisketjon

Production
Peter Mollman

Copy Editor
Barbara Willson

Publicity
Carol Schneider

Cover Illustration: Pater Sato, *Lettering:* Tom Nikosey, Margery Melton (inking), *Photo Retouching:* Charlie Wild, *Color Separations:* Graphic Arts Systems, *Typography:* R S Typographics, *Printing:* Rae Publishing, *Foreword:* Stephen Rosenberg, *Introduction:* John Van Hamersveld

Contents

Foreword

To produce a book on as surprisingly wide a subject as airbrush art is to tempt the fates. By now it is evident that the airbrush is used by contemporary artists of all persuasions, from ''commercial'' to ''fine,'' as a tool of varying importance in their work. Thus to fairly represent the enormous variety and sheer quantity of airbrushing would seem an encyclopedic task.

In order to bring into sharper focus the story of this art form, so unique to our time and culture, we have traced the development of airbrush art through the use of imagery that was, is and will be very familiar to the public. Much of the imagery found in *Airpowered* was commissioned for the purpose of advertising products—be they breakfast cereals, record albums or national news magazines. The artists featured in this book are in demand as problem solvers, conceptualizers and illustrators because they know, above all, how to communicate. In fact, their ability to communicate is so effective that the genre of art appearing in *Airpowered* has become subliminal in the collective awareness of our society.

If, as John Van Hamersveld suggests, the airbrush look is ''Pop art without the cynical point of view,'' then it is more than likely that airbrush art will command a considerably wider audience than the Pop art phenomenon of the sixties. Spend some time with the images in this book. We are convinced that you are looking at the popular art of the eighties.

—Stephen Rosenberg

A Question of A-R-T. Airbrush-rendering is tedious. It is a frustrating, elusive, deceptive, mechanical and laborious job. But amazingly enough, there are professionals who press on into the night like speed demons. While they dream of monetary gains and graphic thrills they delve into the fuzzy clarity of their anxious client's whims. Methodically, they draw, mask and blow the transparent layers of color. Meticulous details become a passive reality and then hyper-reality. Using an airbrush is like playing the violin. It's all in the touch and it's very mesmerizing.

The attraction of the airbrush-rendering is that it reproduces so well. And as a finished product presented to the client it's like a delicious and exotic dessert. A finished rendering has a fine grain in the tints and heavy-stain areas on the paper surface, and the color is so translucent and the density so clear that the result is a very refined image. The delicate shades overlap very lightly to create an evaporative highlighting that just sizzles as a finished piece of work.

The overlapping of color and shading are interesting keys to understanding the quality of the finished image. The technique of layering color shapes requires that each color area be designed and simplified so that it can be worked into a composition. Because of that simplification, the airbrushed image yields easily to becoming a cartooned reality, a fantasy. The application of color is fun, but in between sprays of color is the time-consuming process of cutting masks and waiting for surfaces to dry. Artists spend that down time with the radio or TV, fantasizing while they work and wait. The airbrush artist lives within the game of his imagination, preoccupied with technique, intrigued by the surface and daydreaming with the media.

The airbrush was developed as a photo-retouch tool, as a controllable way of duplicating the surface grain and tones of a photo print. The airbrush artist who has liberated his airbrush from the photographic image, who uses the tool to draw with, has a personal struggle in keeping his independence of style. His attitude and spirit make his work different, and his choice is a major aesthetic decision, his preoccupation as pilot of an illusion. As a history of artists and their solutions to problems of style and technique, *Airpowered* will be encouraging and inspirational to artists looking for ideas. The artists in this book probably started their new work with eyes buzzing to the bright colors and evaporative sprays while their minds zoomed over all the myths and images of our time.

In 1966 I had a dull job in Hollywood. But I found adventure only two blocks away, in the vintage bookstores on exotic Hollywood Boulevard. While my co-workers at Capitol Records were looking at pretty girls to be photographed for album covers, I was looking at Alexey Brodovitch's *Vogue* covers from the 1930s. I couldn't keep my eyes off those covers. The second big surprise to my young eyes was the Bob Dylan portrait by Milton Glaser. To me, a new faith had arrived. I'd never seen a piece with such graphic impact. I thought to myself, "This is the way."

The airbrush was new to us all at that time. Glaser's images would appear from time to time: lines and very bright colors, watercolors and dyes. What was this change coming to graphics...deadly moments. Dave Willardson was in the West and Charlie White was in the East. They were airbrushing inside those Glaseresque lines, using the colorful foggy areas encased within the lines like a soft stained-glass window. I would drift into a daydream, wondering if this was the way.

In late 1969 Bob Zoell airbrushed cartoon characters for the Las Vegas casino Circus, Circus. Foster and Kleiser, the billboard company, had those cartoons hand-painted on magnaboards which towered over Los Angeles. The characters were beautiful shapes with geometrical and fuzzy Cézannesque overlaps; they had a fantastic surface as huge paintings in a gallery of miniatures, little automobiles and people walking about an open-air gallery. I was looking back to Brodovitch, but Bob Zoell was looking at Disney.

From the early seventies I have seen this airbrush phenomenon arrive, and I call it The Media Museum. The merchandising of products on television and in publishing has built an enormous graphic edifice to the Image for Public Consumption, this amazing new world of product fantasies that we live in today. A graphic fantasy, not real but fantastic realism, I guess it's called. It's post–Pop art, without the cynical point of view. Airbrush artists today have made and returned from a voyage to the fantastic—money, time, space and everything to buy into the biggest thing of the decade, The Media Museum.

Seeing these new artists and art directors on a graphic rampage over the last decade, as beginners at one end and as successful professionals on the other, has been a wonderful insight into the times. Their fame reflects a contemporary sense of the artist so soon popular but without the grace of an endorsement by the intelligentsia of the times. These people who participate in The Media Museum have a new kind of sophistication. They understand desire.

You can see in *Airpowered* that these new artists work with and are influenced by the nostalgic, eclectic and plagiaristic view of historical and contemporary art that pervades the commercial sensibility. They have looked into, played with, examined and participated in the development of each other's work, attempting to go one better. I think this loose collaboration causes their individual styles to date. But now, at the end of this decade, we will see another generation in hot pursuit, searching for their visual answer to the eternal graphic question—the void—that will always create new interpretations of the airbrush style.

—John Van Hamersveld

History

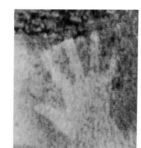

PREHISTORY: THE LAYING ON OF HANDS   History, it is generally agreed, begins with the deliberate recording of facts. Thus our cave-dwelling ancestors, due to their lack of systematic record keeping, are deemed prehistoric. Yet their wall art is a historical reality: these mystifying signs and symbols, paintings and engravings provide scholars with at least as many questions as answers and are the earliest evidence of the human need to communicate, decorate and worship. They are also the earliest instance of airbrush art. While necessarily a primitive form of the literal definition of airbrushing, the principle of creating an image by spraying pigment onto a surface was originated by the first practicing artists to inhabit the earth.

A recurring image in the ancient caves of Lascaux and Pech-Merle in southwestern France is the "negative hand," which is believed to have been of magical significance. Very much like a child's first outline, these images were rendered by covering part of the wall's surface with the hand and painting the unprotected area around the hand. Experts have concluded that the color surrounding these hands was most likely sprayed through a primitive blower, probably fashioned of bone. Thus an art form that today is often criticized for being too mechanical began as an oral, hence rather personal, technique.

Annette Laming, in her respected analysis of cave art at Lascaux, remarks: "The artists of Lascaux knew of and used a process rarely employed in other painted caves: they were able to produce a blurred effect for a contour or a filling-in and use it in conjunction with clear and precise brush strokes. Nothing is known of the actual process, but it is believed to have consisted of a technique of applying powdered pigment by means of a primitive type of spray gun."

Phrases such as "primitive blower" and "sprayed pigment" repeatedly occur in treatises on cave art, and there is no doubt that the method described is one of the oldest techniques in art. Indeed, origins are the *least* controversial issue in the history of the airbrush. Alternately condemned as a "parasite" and lauded as "a medium which can meet almost any demand made on it," the airbrush has rarely been a matter of indifference.

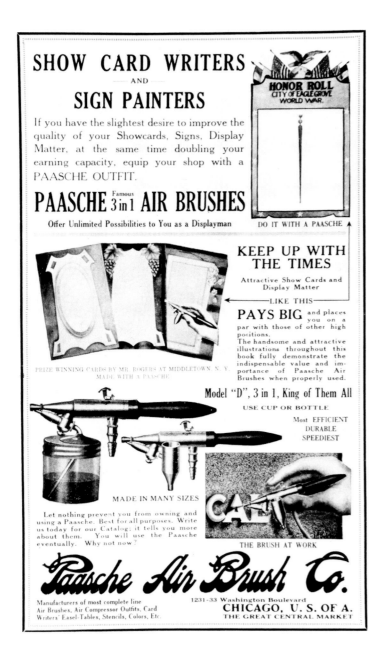
THE AIRBRUSH   Although the principle of air-powered painting has existed since people first produced art, the actual date of the invention of the airbrush is unknown. A United States patent for an airbrush case design, however, indicates that the airbrush, as we know it today, has been in use since at least 1888.

Similar in size and shape to a fountain pen, the airbrush sprays pigment onto a surface without ever touching the surface itself. It should not be confused with a spray gun, which conveys great amounts of color to broad surfaces. At the tip of the airbrush is a small nozzle, through which paint is pulled by compressed air. The airbrush is connected to its air supply by a thin rubber hose, and the paint to be used is stored in a small cup attached to the side of the brush.

Because of its fine size, the airbrush can best accommodate watercolors thinned to the consistency of waterproof ink; heavier pigments, obviously, would clog the works. The spray is distinctively delicate, particularly adept at producing fine lines and subtle shadings of tone. But the airbrush can also produce a broader spray, as is often done when rendering backgrounds, by increasing the volume of air; an adjustable valve controls the proportion of air to paint, which allows the operator to vary the quality of the spray.

One of the basic misconceptions about the airbrush is that it is used only for photo retouching. Although initially perceived as a retouching implement, the airbrush was soon recognized as an artist's tool with specific, if numerous capabilities and characteristics.

Primarily, since the brush itself never touches the paper, the artist's presence need not be felt beyond subject and design. A distant cousin of the camera in its ability to duplicate reality, the airbrush produces a soft, sleek and smooth look with clean, sharp edges. And because there are no brush strokes, this tool, with its unrivaled ability to create subtle shades and highlights, is also perfect for rendering imaginary worlds, unencumbered by any recognizable human imprint.

The airbrush can be used in a variety of ways for a variety of purposes. Some artists, such as Doug Johnson, apply paint with it as an underpainting and then develop the work with other techniques, while others use it for finishing touches, as Vargas does when he softens an already completed watercolor with his airbrush. The following list, compiled between 1915 and 1920, and published in *A Treatise on the Airbrush* (1930), provides an idea of various applications of the instrument at that early date.

Artists Commercial retouching, magazine covers, heraldry, colouring of prints, engravings, etchings, etc., portraits, miniatures, artificial flowers; *Architects* Colouring maps, bird's-eye views; *Book binding* Tinting, varnishing; *China decorators* Backgrounds, designs; *Campaign buttons* Tinting; *Decorators* Interiors, mural and otherwise; *Dyers* For applying dyes to fabric without affecting the rest of the cloth; *Engravers; Enameling* Wood or iron products; *Fancy goods* Tinting or spraying on designs; *Feathers* Tinting or dyeing; *Fans* Tinting or dyeing; *Frame makers* Staining moulding, gilding frames, colouring or gilding mats;

Samuel D. Otis   1928

Jewelry manufacturers Tinting, lacquering; *Leather*
Dyeing, enameling, gilding, finishing; *Laces*
Colouring; *Miniatures; Picture mats; Photo colouring; Portrait finishing; Parchment shades; Slippers;
Toys: Vases and pottery.* The obvious versatility is
nevertheless restricted to the mere touching-up, though *A
Manual of Airbrush Technique* (1946) notes a number of
more creative uses:
Architectural drawings Because of its special ability to
render shades and highlights, the airbrush is desirable for
representing different kinds of building materials; *Fashion illustrations* For the same reason, it is excellent in
rendering textile fabrics, recognizable by their interplay
with light; *Show cards* Airbrushed borders and lettering
were effective in giving a card distinction.
It should be mentioned here that show cards were com-
monly displayed by merchants long before the days
of advertising agencies. Airbrushed show cards were very
popular as early as 1912.
    S. Ralph Maurello's *The Complete Airbrush Book*

was published in 1955 and is proof of a vast expansion in
both popularity and variety. By dividing the uses of the
airbrush into the categories of Rendering and Retouching, the
book includes in the former such creative applications
as posters and illustrations, mechanical and technical illustration, and general design. Thus, in the forty years between
1915 and 1955, the airbrush had come of age and was no
longer regarded only as a tool for the photo retoucher; like
the handbrush, the sculptor's chisel and the camera,
it had achieved legitimacy as a tool of the artist's trade.
This book is a record of the unique and significant
achievement of this tool.

    THE AIRBRUSH AND PHOTOGRAPHY   In 1839
the daguerreotype, precursor of the camera, was invented,
and suddenly the physical world could be reproduced with
the snap of a shutter. It's not hard to imagine why many
painters felt threatened; a new kind of artist, the photographer, could compete in the market for pictures and
portraits.

George B. Petty 1906

As mentioned above, the patent for the airbrush case is recorded with the U.S. Patent Office in the year 1888—forty-nine years after the first daguerreotype was developed. It is obvious that the airbrush itself preceded the case designed to hold it; further, it is reasonable to assume that the earliest photographers, hindered by the relatively crude reproductive facilities of early photographic methods, had the desire to retouch their work. A likely conclusion is that the Victorian era, with its proclivity for a picturesque realism, initiated the partnership of camera and airbrush, and that the means of retouching photographs is nearly as old as photography itself.

Alberto Vargas, whose Vargas Girl is known throughout the world, first picked up an airbrush in 1898. And he recalls that years before that, while he was growing up in a small village in Peru, his father was using an airbrush to retouch photographs. Charlie Wild, who runs a retouching studio in Los Angeles, remembers seeing a picture of someone getting compressed air from a bicycle pump for a retouching job. He also remembers his father using an airbrush for retouching. "I bet it's been around since the Civil War," he ventures. "Look at those color-tint pictures of Lincoln—there was no color photography in those days."

One color that depended on photo retouching was yellow—as in "yellow journalism," a phrase that originated when the first color comic-strip cartoon, The Yellow Kid, ran in a New York newspaper called *The World.* Appearing in 1895 in a paper known for the provocative nature of its reportage, this early experiment in color printing came to be associated with the phenomenon of sensationalism. "They'd hire actors to re-enact famous crimes and scandals," Charlie Wild recalls. "The photographer would record the 'scene of the crime,' and then the retoucher would brush out the actors' faces and replace them with the faces of the actual people involved." It is doubtful that forwarding the cause of scandal did much to give airbrushing a good name.

There are many viable reasons for retouching a photograph. You might think of those unsightly blemishes that were mercifully removed from your graduation picture. But the more practical instances of retouching involve the reproduction of photographs in newspapers, magazines and other printed matter.

With the invention in 1874 of a printing process called the halftone, it became possible to reproduce photographs, and the *London Illustrated Weekly* began to do so in the late nineteenth century. Though a technical description of complex printing processes is not necessary for our purposes, the reader will readily perceive the difference in quality between a photograph reproduced in a newspaper, where the lines of the letterpress are easily discernible, and one reproduced in a magazine, where the finer reproductive

process of photogravure is generally employed. The airbrush is an essential tool in both.

Of retouching for newspapers, Maurello observed in *Commercial Art Techniques:* "Since the coarse screen of the newspaper and the type of paper used do not hold the rather subtle distinctions of tones or fine lines that may appear in a photograph, retouching for newspaper reproduction entails a bolder and more definite treatment."

A different printing process, rotogravure, is widely used in Sunday supplements and magazines (which helps to explain Irving Berlin's lyric "And you'll find that you're in the rotogravure," in "Easter Parade"). In his *Handbook of Advertising and Printing,* Carl Greer noted: "In rotogravure printing, a great range of tone is obtained. The reproduction is not made up of lines and dots, as in letterpress, but is composed of an ink film of wide variation and depth. It is by this means that a richness and artistic effect attained by no other means is secured." With the "lines and dots" eliminated through the rotogravure process, the airbrush, with its ability to render smooth and "stippleless" illustrations, became a perfect instrument both for retouching photographs and for creating original art that would reproduce well. Thus the English designer Stanley Corthine wrote in 1933: "In photogravure the use of the air-brush shows to a great advantage. The even and graduated tones obtainable with the air-brush are ideally suited to the beautiful photographic reproduction of this process."

That photography had a profound effect on the development of airbrush technique is apparent. But there were other, more far-reaching influences at work—namely, society's changing attitude toward, and eventual acceptance of, the machine as an integral part of culture. The airbrush, itself a kind of machine, can attribute its emergence as an artistic medium to the forces that brought about that change.

THE AIRBRUSH COMES INTO ITS OWN   By 1920 the airbrush was widely used as a retouching tool and show-card implement, and was recognized for its suitability to the new photo-reproduction processes. Another machine that made remarkable gains in popularity during the twenties was the automobile. Technology, manifest in the complexity and speed of the automobile, became a cause célèbre among intellectuals and artists and in the business world; whether to reject or embrace its ramifications was hotly debated throughout Europe and America. And once the car became available to the general public, the choice was not simply whether to buy one, but which one to buy. Thus the automobile turned advertising into a major industry. And the clean, sharp and accessible images and lettering of which the airbrush was capable would play an important part in this advertising revolution.

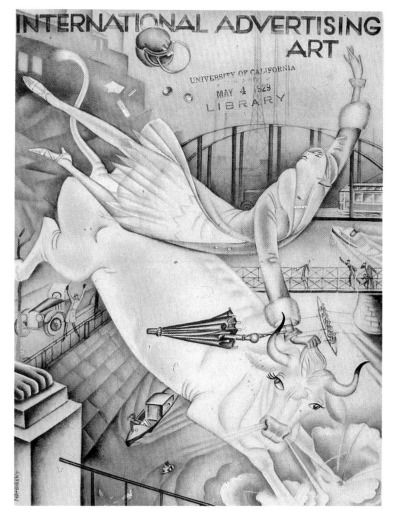

N. Brodsky 1929

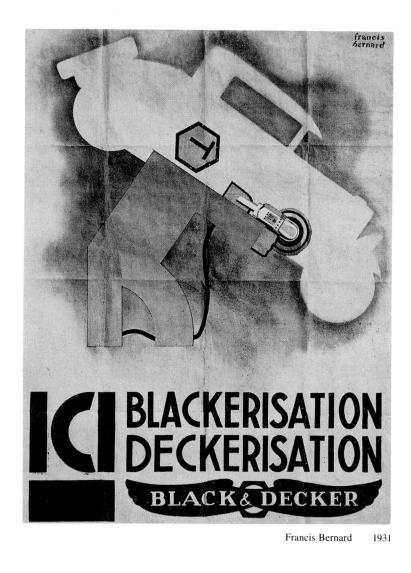

Francis Bernard 1931

GERMANY: THE BAUHAUS   The artistic movement that was absolutely central to the acceptance of the new technology originated in Weimar, Germany. Determined to bring some order to the chaos that was loosely termed "modern art"—Futurism, Cubism, post-Impressionism, Expressionism—a group of artists joined together with the express intention of forming a "new artist."

The Bauhaus opened in 1919, under the direction of the architect Walter Gropius. Dedicated to synthesizing art with economics, creativity with technology, and aesthetics with craftsmanship, this remarkable school condemned the distinction between fine and applied arts and dismissed the romantic notion of the artist as outcast. These passé beliefs were replaced at the Bauhaus with a commitment to communication that would gradually lead to the integration of art and society. Gropius proclaimed: "The old dualistic world-concept which envisaged the ego in opposition to the universe is rapidly losing ground. . . . No longer can anything exist in isolation. . . . So long as machine economy remains an end in itself rather than a means of freeing the

intellect from the burden of mechanical labor, the individual will remain enslaved and society will remain disordered." Eminent artists flocked to the Bauhaus, eager to participate in this revolutionary movement. Kandinsky, Moholy-Nagy and Paul Klee served on the faculty, experimenting with such new forms as photomontage, and developed the concept of graphic design and layout. The Bauhaus was, according to the art historian Alan M. Fern, "the single most influential force of its decade; it was an institution with which every designer had to agree or fight. It was practically impossible, at least in Europe, to ignore. . ."

Moholy-Nagy, who taught the photography course, is considered an early proponent of photomontage in poster art. With the growth of advertising, the poster became a major means of promotion, for which the main objective was communication. "A poster," wrote Moholy-Nagy, "must convey instantaneously all the high points of an idea. The greatest possibilities for future development lie in the proper use of photographic means. . . techniques:

22

Colmena   1931

Henry Ehlers   1932

Herbert Bayer   1931

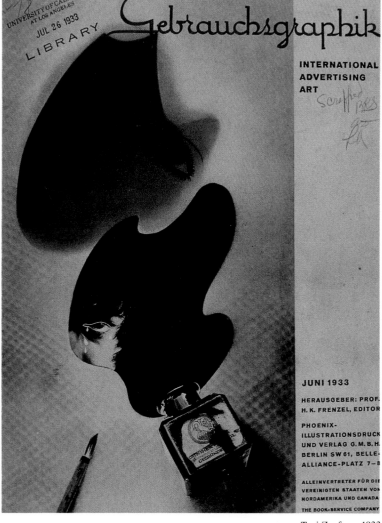

Toni Zepf   1933

The impact of the Bauhaus cannot be emphasized too much. All the world over, students and established artists alike recognized the possibilities of this new approach to art. An important example is *E. McKnight Kauffer,* an American who was working in England when the Bauhaus began and whose self-education was soon given a mighty boost by the philosophies of this movement.

Born in Montana in 1890, Kauffer dropped out of school in the eighth grade to follow his artistic impulses. His first job was as a scene painter for a traveling theater company, which eventually landed him in San Francisco; there he changed jobs to work in a bookstore, where he devoured the art history section. In 1912 he visited Europe, and he would remain there for most of his working life.

Settling in London after brief stays in Munich and Paris, Kauffer was discovered by Frank Pick, director of the newly opened advertising department of the London Underground. Pick responded enthusiastically to the imaginative use of Cubism that Kauffer had achieved on his first

well-known poster, "A Flight of Birds," and immediately commissioned him to produce a series of travel posters for the subways. For the workers who struggled daily through rush-hour commuting, Pick wanted to provide idyllic and restful travel scenes. Kauffer's posters, many of which were airbrushed, conveyed this tranquillity in the midst of work-a-day bustle and, in fact, were so well received that Winston Churchill himself expressed his appreciation to the artist.

Along with Cassandre in France, Kauffer is often mentioned as the first person to bring symbolism to poster art—to advertise with forms symbolic of a product instead of depicting the product itself. In this, as in his blending of word and image, the Bauhaus influence is evident. In 1921 Kauffer returned to the United States in hopes of "selling" this approach to his own country. His efforts met with dismal failure, and he returned to England and continued success. Ironically, in 1937 he was the first advertising artist to be given a retrospective at New York's Museum of Modern

Pierra Masseau 1931

Charles Angrave 1932

Art. Upon Kauffer's death in 1954, T. S. Eliot said of him: "He did something for modern art with the public as well as doing something for the public with modern art."

FRANCE: ART DECO   By the mid-twenties, the acceptance of advertising and the abandonment of individual for collective artistry that began at the Bauhaus had traveled to France. Though most French art workshops still adhered strictly to the right angles and objectivity of Picasso's Cubism, the growing desire among merchants to communicate with the public through art brought about the marriage of Cubist simplicity and appealing ornamentation, which together formed the style known as Art Deco. Characterized by geometric patterns in graceful relationship, the linear design of Deco made it a style for which the airbrush was perfectly suited.

A. M. Cassandre (born Adolphe Mouron) produced the first significant poster art of the period. His influential

style, in keeping with the new age of advertising, was dynamic and accessible, aesthetically flawless and immediately arresting. "Since a poster is a way of addressing a hurried passer-by already harassed by a jumble of images of every kind," he said, "it must provoke surprise, rape his sensibility and mark his memory with an indelible imprint. An ingenious idea capable of striking the passer-by is not enough; the right way of expressing the idea must be found; brutality perhaps, but also style."

One of those swept up in the revolutionary concepts of advertising was the Russian refugee *Alexey Brodovitch*. The agitated atmosphere of experimentation over the Paris art world was for him a welcome contrast to the violent revolution that had utterly changed his homeland. Brodovitch thrived in Paris, where he had found work as a set painter for the Ballet Russe. The company's founder and director was Sergei Diaghilev, often noted as an inspiration of modern art. Diaghilev's concepts of unity and form were catalysts for Brodovitch's early ideas, and it is likely that the impresario's role as mentor had an influence

Alexey Brodovitch   1930

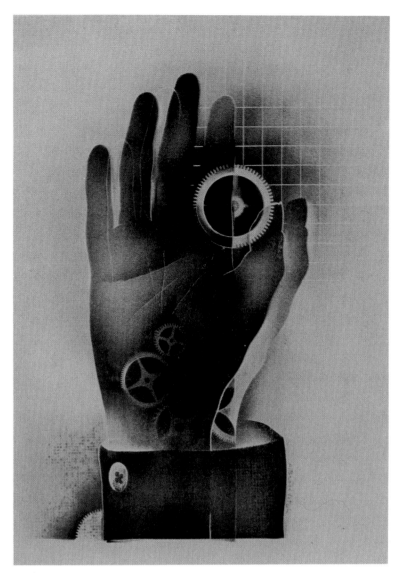

Alexey Brodovitch 1930

on Brodovitch's later emergence as philosopher-teacher.

After Brodovitch won a poster competition, his graphic design attained international respect, and the biggest Parisian shops competed for his services as art director. All of this despite his insistence on experimentation, which is evident in his statement on artist's materials: "Industrial lacquers, airbrush, a thin ray of light, perfected hard, flexible steel needles, surgical knives and even dental implements may take the place of water colours, indurable and clumsy brushes and charcoal pens and crayons."

In 1934 Brodovitch began his twenty-five-year tenure as art director of *Harper's Bazaar* and soon attracted such avid protégés as Irving Penn, Cartier Bresson, Jean Cocteau, Richard Avedon and Saul Steinberg. The philosopher A. N. Whitehead wrote: "In his personal aesthetic, Brodovitch lived for change. Each editorial achievement was a fact, repetition was banality. *Harper's Bazaar,* in short, became a center for the most fertile minds in editorial visual communication."

The full flower of French airbrush poster art is perhaps seen in the work of *Jean Carlu.* A precise draftsman,

Carlu was studying architectural design when an accident led to the amputation of his right arm—his drawing arm. He was eighteen years old. He spent his recuperative time productively: taking stock of the world around him, Carlu realized how adamantly he opposed war and violence, and he gradually trained himself to draw with his left hand. The two activities combined in his commitment to poster art that, whenever possible, would be devoted to the cause of peace.

In harmony with Bauhaus philosophy, Carlu had no reservations about doing commercial art. As an article written in 1935 noted: "Carlu sees no obstacle to art in its being thus harnessed to a purpose. A proof of this is his conception of mediaeval art, which he regards as the creation of clerical propaganda. Art is always a most valuable form of propaganda for an idea, imbued with special content; only the clients change. Centuries ago the church was the client, now commerce and the state have taken its place."

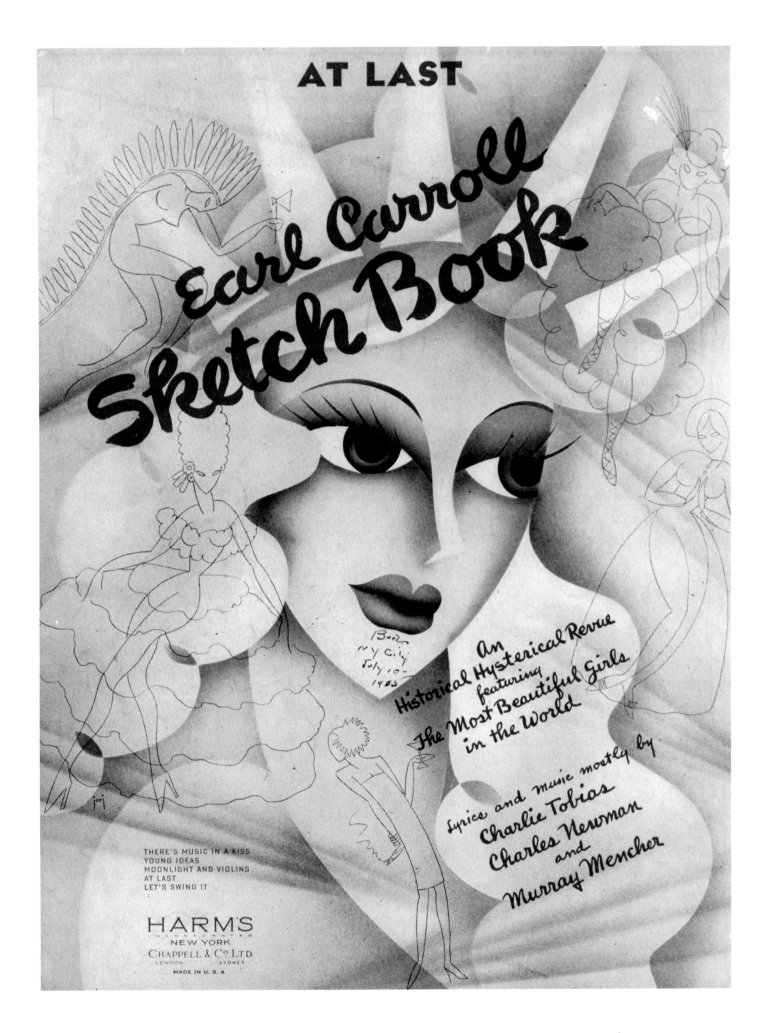

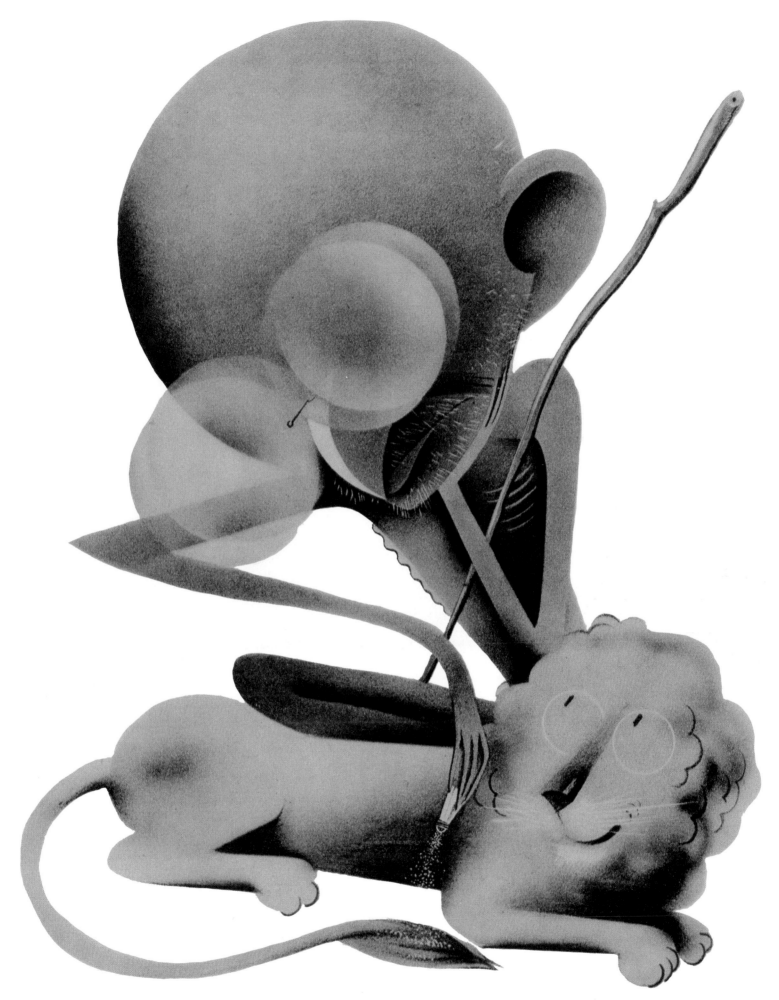

Gandhi, The Tail-Salter

Garretto   1930

33

Joseph Binder   1937

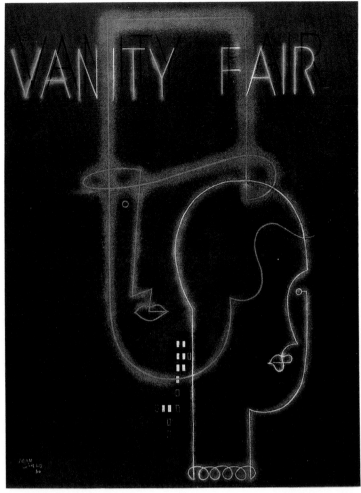

Jean Carlu   1931

Whether propagandizing for peace or advertising a product, Carlu's work is marked by symbolism and an exactness of execution that is almost scientific. That his vision was aided by the airbrush is clear in Alan M. Fern's observation: "These posters seem to bear no mark of the designer's hand; colors and shapes either end precisely or flow off in utterly smooth gradations."

Meanwhile, in Vienna, a confident young artist had also applied his gifts to the poster. *Joseph Binder* later recalled, "I did not want to become a 'Number-Two Picasso.' I would rather become a 'Number-One Designer of Posters.'" He was, in fact, one of the first poster artists to receive international recognition, and most of his work was done entirely in airbrush. Indeed, it is very likely that Binder was the first pure airbrush artist.

Like Germany, Vienna in the early twenties was still recovering from the devastation of World War I; understandably, there was a national impulse toward achieving a sense of order. Technology, and the speed and efficiency of which a machine was capable, seemed a convincing solu-

tion to the chaos. As we have seen, along with the machine came advertising, and with advertising came posters. The advent of the latter was sudden, as Carla Binder (the artist's wife) explains: "The profession of the poster artist was so new when Binder began in the early 1920's that his mother did not know how to explain to her friends what it was her son was doing for a living."

What he was doing was laying the groundwork for contemporary graphic design, the natural child of the poster. Like Cassandre, Carlu and the Bauhaus masters, Binder was thoroughly schooled in printing techniques, having served an apprenticeship with a publishing house in Vienna; and like his "comrades," Binder was intent on contributing to the new artform. "A new artform is developing," he wrote, "graphic design for advertising, which is different from any other artform. As an organic part of our time conception, it must be synchronized with the increased speed of present life and civilization. [Because] the eye [is] capable of registering [at] the speed of lightning...the sales story has to be told pictorially for quick and lasting impressions."

35

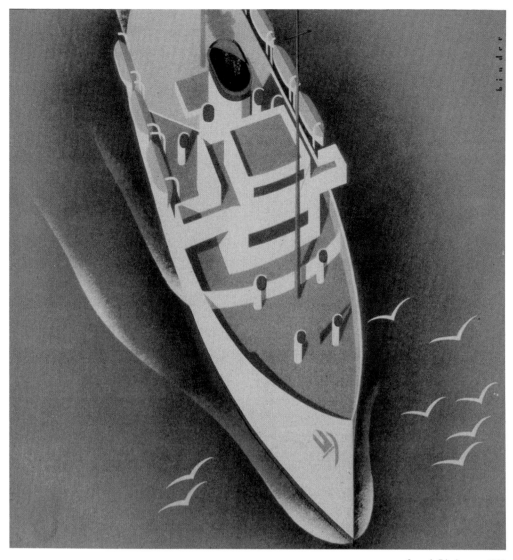

Joseph Binder   1931

For his medium, he often chose the airbrush. By nature a perfectionist, he had the will and patience that the instrument required. "The artist cannot live by man-made time," he said. "Due to my technical education, I have to render everything with precision." As for subject matter, "A design will be most attractive when it gives the essentials in a concentrated form. The essentials of bodies are the basic form."

In addition to his pictorial work, Binder became an expert designer of trademarks and logos. Using the airbrush in much the same way that show-card designers had at the beginning of the century, he established the look with which numerous companies, products and storefronts were associated. In 1922, at the age of twenty-four, he opened his own studio. And in 1928 his posters were published in an international collection of graphic art, *Gebrauchsgraphik.* In this publication Binder was described as "the strongest talent and greatest hope of Austrian commercial art . . . a born poster artist. . . . All his work is, both artistically and graphically speaking, keenly thought out

and reduced to the most concentrated form and incomparable in its effect." This exposure expanded his already considerable reputation, and many commercial artists from around the world traveled to visit his studio. One of them, Otis Shepard, was to become the first major airbrush artist in the United States.

Though Binder enjoyed teaching, his decision to organize his ideas into a formalized course of instruction was the result of what might be called an occupational hazard. The correct position for airbrush work involves placing the arm on the table so that the elbow rests a few inches from the table edge; the elbow remains fixed at this spot and only the forearm moves swinging side to side as the work progresses. This is intense and exacting work, demanding both in mental and physical concentration. In 1932 Binder was diagnosed as having "tennis elbow" and ordered by his doctor to keep his right arm in a sling for the summer months. This enforced layoff led to his first stint as a teacher, which in turn led to an invitation the following year to give courses in design in the United States.

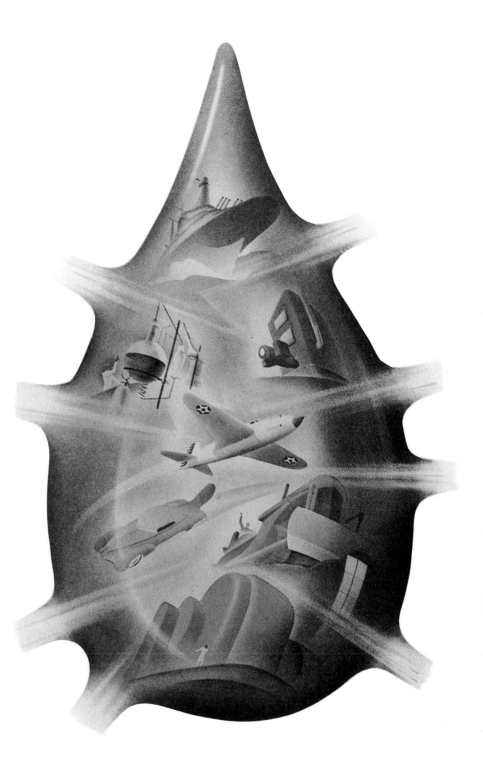

Given Binder's enormous and long-lived success as both artist and teacher, his influence on commercial art is nearly incalculable. Not surprisingly, his concepts are often echoed by the contemporary artists whose work appears in this book. His impact on American artists was immediate, for his arrival in 1933 coincided with an unprecedented blossoming of the nation's youngest industry: advertising.

ADVERTISING ART IN THE THIRTIES   The advent of two major institutions marked the expansion of advertising: the advertising agency and the popular picture magazine. With hundreds of new products on the market, companies could no longer handle the volume of their own publicity, so agencies were formed for that purpose. And what better vehicle for promoting a product than a magazine over which consumers could linger at their own pace?

The experimentation that characterized twenties art had by 1930 mellowed into maturity, adopting an air of sophistication and elegance. It has been suggested that the cool reserve of graphic design in the thirties was a reaction to the increased political turbulence of the times; this seems a possible explanation of the singularly controlled and classical lines of the "New Objectivity," which informed the range of the visual arts—fashion, architecture, posters, and magazine advertising.

Ted Hawkins 1938

Pettrocelli   1938

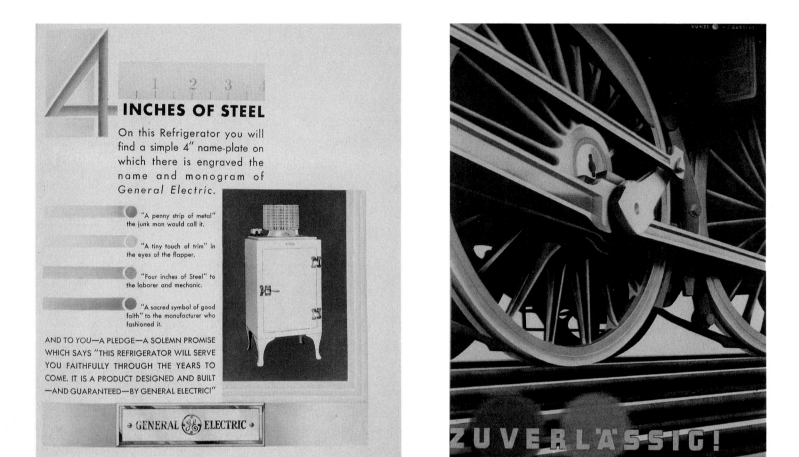

Willi Kunze   1938

The Aviation Trinity

OVERHEAD is the flash of wings. The air is alive with man-made thunder. Ten thousand tense spectators crane their necks as a plane rounds the final pylon—and roars home to victory.

Of such stuff is the drama of air racing—a drama which draws an increasing gallery of the air-minded every year. Yet behind the thrills and the spectacle is solid, scientific purpose. For America's air races and air meets are, in effect, the proving ground of the inseparable trinity of aviation—*pilots, planes* and *petroleum*.

Out of a long background of testing in these speed trials have come Gulf's Aviation Products.

In the fastest conveyances built by man, they have given a noteworthy account of themselves. Last year, many different planes, piloted by many different men, piled up an amazing total of victories for one fuel and one lubricant—Gulf.

At the 1935 National Air Races, 8 out of the 11 winners used Gulf, and at the 1935 All-American Air Meet, Gulf won 8 out of 9 events, as well as setting 2 world's records and a national record. Such triumphs as these are potent evi-

dence of Gulf's leadership in the realm of aviation.

And, when you make your next flight to some distant city, there is a good chance that your giant transport will come to rest under the very shadow of the familiar Orange Disc. For Gulf serves many of the major airports in its territory, and powers the ships of many of America's leading airlines.

To all who use petroleum products, these facts are significant. For they indicate the high standards of performance which have come to be associated with the Gulf name. *Gulf Oil Corporation of Pennsylvania . . . Gulf Refining Company.*

★ ★ ★ **GULF** ★ ★ ★

41

Airbrush illustration first appeared in the *New York Art Director's Annual* in 1928; the artist was *Samuel T. Otis*. But the first American illustrator to make the airbrush poster a popular form of advertising art was *Otis Shepard*.

As noted above, Shepard had visited Joseph Binder's Vienna studio in the late twenties. He was obviously impressed by what he saw. Shepard's airbrushed posters for Wrigley's chewing gum recall Binder's insistence on "quick and lasting impressions" and fast became a familiar sight on America's avenues and roadways; and beyond promoting a product, they have come to be recognized as genuine Americana in their own right. Shepard had strong feelings about advertising illustration and took his job as Wrigley's publicity designer very seriously indeed. As one article said, "At least twelve hours a day he thinks, talks and chews Wrigley's. He believes that to sell the public a product in posters the artist must not only know his product intimately but that he must also possess an understanding of what interests the public and compels it to read. Consequently, people in all walks of life are contacted. Office employees, elevator operators, labourers, taxi drivers, waiters and children from the slums to Park Avenue occupy the field of Shepard's research."

With at least as much fervor as he used to sell chewing gum, "Shep" sought to replace the "pretty-girl posters" that cluttered the nation's view with his new look. He abhorred the lack of faith in public taste that was held by the business world, and regarded Kauffer, Carlu and Cassandre as designers whose work could be understood and appreciated by everyone. In his writing, Shepard argued against the patronizing attitudes of the advertising agency and advocated an imaginative approach to advertising design, convinced that modern graphics would be received by Americans as they had been by Europeans. "After all," he explained, "the appeal of a real poster is basic. Its simple language of pictorial symbols should carry a message to the most primitive person. The primitive and savage peoples in their art embodied the principles of the finest poster design."

In citing "primitives," Kauffer and Carlu, Shepard traced, albeit unwittingly, the progress of airbrushing from the cave artists of Lascaux to his contemporaries. Shepard himself used the airbrush almost exclusively, and the art he created with it was not only accepted by the American public, but also became a visual trademark of the cool, slick thirties.

Working hand in hand, the ad agency and the new fashion magazines catered to the sophistication of the affluent members of society. It is evident that the agencies had begun to acknowledge the public's aesthetic appreciation of simplicity and the "New Objectivity," whose recognition was due in large part to the pioneering efforts of *Vogues'* art director, Mehemed Fehmy Agha.

Of Russian-Turkish extraction, Agha brought to American publishing the elegance and maturity of Europe (as Brodovitch would five years later). In addition to a thorough knowledge of languages, science and technology, Agha had a keen visual sense. Credited with changing the look of magazine layout, he is attributed with having conceived of the pictorial feature. A contemporary article stated: "[He] set up and conducted complicated engineering experiments in an effort to give the artist and photographer a printed page in color that was worthy of the art that graced it." It is no wonder that many renowned artists wanted to work with him. Nor is it difficult to see Agha's influence in such magazines as *Fortune* and *Harper's Bazaar.* Together with *Vogue* and *Vanity Fair,* these publications became the arbiters of taste at home and abroad. Once introduced to the simplicity and graceful contours of the new look, the public could not get enough of it.

Airbrush art flourished during this period. Appearing on the covers and in the pages of these magazines was the work of Carlu, Binder and many others. Noteworthy for his airbrushed caricatures is Italian-born *Paolo Garretto*.

Like others who were attracted to the precision-demanding medium, Garretto had a technical background, having trained to become an engineer. While studying art in Rome, he is said to have become an enthusiastic Fascist; his political caricatures, some of which were published in the Fascist paper *J'Impero,* became the rage in Europe and, later, in the United States. Garretto's style evidently superseded his politics, and before long he was a frequent contributor to the elite periodicals mentioned above.

Whether of Chaplin or Mussolini, his caricatures blend image and essence, and thus capture the personality instead of simply distorting a face; the subject's feelings, ideology and character are laid bare, and as only airbrush work can, Garretto's images seem to float on the page, like balloons blown up for the reader's enjoyment. A 1947 edition of *Graphis* summarized his unique achievement: "Under his hands persons become moving puppets, in an atmosphere that no longer smells of typography or of paper, pen and inkstand. Colour itself becomes abstract by a pure relationship of tones, continually renewing the festival of their clashes. Garretto's drawings might really be called coloured, plastic monuments . . . marvellous surrealistic toys for adults."

JULY

PRICE 35 CTS.
©THE CONDÉ NAST
PUBLICATIONS, INC.
1 9 3 3
★

Garretto   1933

Peace Time Warrior   President Paul Von Hindenburg 1932

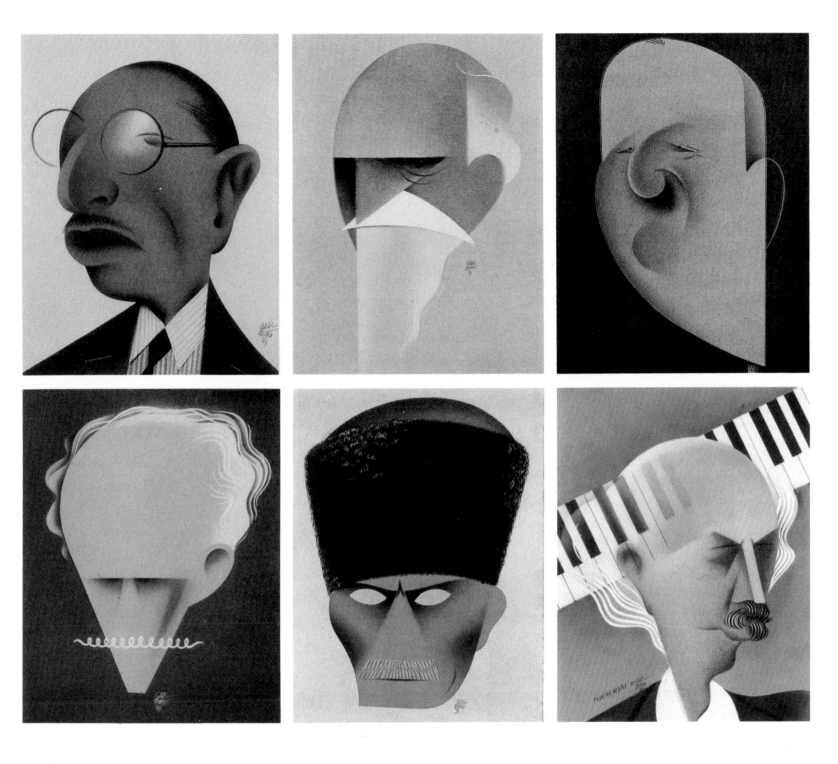

by Garretto

Olympian of the Musical Sphere
Stravinsky 1934

World Financier
The Right Honourable
  Montagu Collet Norman 1931

World Financier
Minister of Finance
Pierre Etienne Flaudin 1931

Olympian of the Musical Sphere
Toscanini 1934

Peace Time Warrior
Dictator Mastopha Kemal Pasha 1932

Olympian of the Musical Sphere 1934
Paderewski

Sure C-A-L-L me back in T-E-N M-I-N-U-T-E-S

George Petty 1938

"RUNNING IMPROVES MY FIGURE? — SILLY, IT'S JUST MY JANTZEN!"

George Petty 1939

For pleasure-seeking Americans in a world on the brink of war, show business became the major avenue of escape. In the razzle-dazzle of the *Ziegfeld Follies* and the glamour of Hollywood, beautiful women and lilting melodies wooed audiences from daily concerns; even the Depression could be temporarily forgotten. The pretty girls of *George Petty* became a national pastime through the pages of *Esquire*. But it was *Alberto Vargas'* Varga Girl that came to represent female perfection from Ziegfeld to Hollywood, *Esquire* to *Playboy*. Both men utilized the air-brush to highlight the beauty of the American woman and, indeed, the Varga Girl became the ultimate symbol of home to the boys and men fighting overseas.

Anton   1941

THE WAR YEARS   "Nothing is easier than leading the people on a leash. I just hold up a dazzling campaign poster and they jump through it." Thus spake Joseph Goebbels. In *Mein Kampf,* Hitler himself noted the importance of posters in forming public opinion. Thus for the first time in any country, a Ministry for Popular Enlightenment and Propaganda was established as a separate government agency of the Third Reich.

Although a number of excellent posters had come out of World War I, the advances made in graphic art between the wars had bestowed unprecedented significance on visual information. Through posters, consumer magazines and pinups, masses of people were bound together by their increased appreciation for the printed picture.

IN 2 TAGEN NACH NORD-AMERIKA!
DEUTSCHE ZEPPELIN-REEDEREI

Jupp Wiertz   1937

Weiner Purrell   1942

Abram Games

While the staggering quantity of Nazi poster art was nothing if not lacking in subtlety, the work of the English artist *Abram Games* combined impact with artistry. Often cited as the outstanding poster artist of World War II, Games was in fact so well known by 1940 that upon enlisting in the British army, he was summoned to the War Office to serve as a poster designer. Most of his posters were instructional, and like all of his work, distinguished by a profound concern for the message that they conveyed. Because Games so obviously cared, so did the viewer; and because his craft matched his involvement, his message was effectively internalized and executed.

''The discipline of reason conditions the expression of design, stimulates and guides, remains the final test,'' Games wrote. ''The designer constructs, winds the spring. The viewer's eye is caught, the spring released. The message is home and interest excited.'' His skill at translating message into striking image is plainly seen in his posters that encourage blood donations or aid for the homeless and the blind, in which there is an emotional intimacy that cannot be ignored. ''His technical mastery of his craft—his airbrush work particularly—'' *Graphis* remarked in 1947, ''is evident in every corner of his designs,'' and it was this mastery that enabled Games to rouse and comfort the English populace throughout the war.

Sevek   1945

Several of the artists already discussed did war covers
and ads for the major magazines. Attracted by the high
standards of these publications, serious designers were
eager to have their work displayed on a *Vogue* cover or in
an ad in *Harper's Bazaar.* The *Fortune* covers of the war
period were particularly noteworthy, not least for their frequent use of airbrush art. Many of them were the work of
George Giusti. His forte was the pictorial representation of
technological processes, a task for which the airbrush—
itself a technological process for painting pictures—was
both well suited and appropriate. Giusti's illustrations
furthered public understanding of the rapidly changing
world by expressing complex procedures in a simple and
direct style that imparted a reassuring sense of security to a
nation in dire need.

HE TALKED · THEY DIED

Abram Games   1943

The troops abroad, however, needed more than security; they needed something that would make them feel good. The airbrush-enhanced Petty and Varga Girls did just that. And with the first Varga Girl calendar in 1940, an industry was born. The pinup girl became big business. After the war she found herself transplanted from the fighter plane to the living room, and over thirty years later is still enjoyed. Though mores have allowed blatant expression of what could once only be hinted at, and though what then could only be painted may now be photographed, the airbrushed pinup has remained popular—as devotees of the Vargas Girl in *Playboy* will witness.

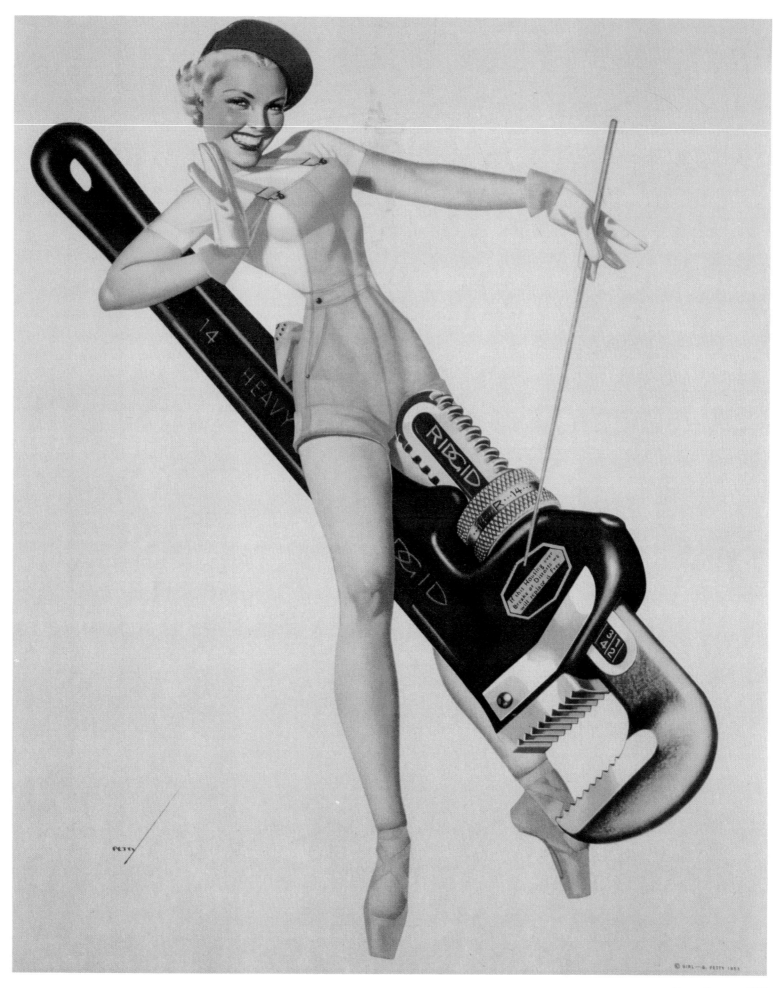

George Petty   1953

George Petty   1943

George Petty

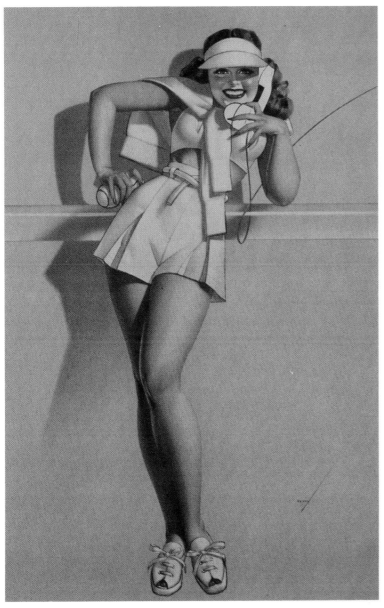

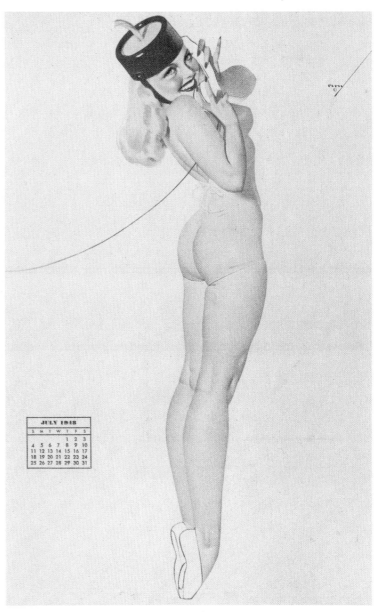

George Petty

George Petty   1948

Pinocchio 1939

60

Peter Pan 1953

Fantasia 1940

Fantasia 1940

In 1939, the most expensive animated feature film to date was released. At $2.6 million, *Pinocchio* was the brainchild of Walt Disney, who put his every creative idea and innovative technique into the film. According to *Film Comment,* "He conducted story meetings, reviewed animation, watched test reels of color footage. He changed backgrounds, altered animated air-brush effects, and even made the decisions on which highlights were to be sprayed or brushed on characters."

Pinocchio was the first animated film to make heavy use of airbrush. The recently invented multiplane camera, which created the illusion of depth in animation, also created all sorts of difficulties, chief among them inconsistent lighting. Disney found that the airbrush, with its unique ability to create subtle gradations in light, was the answer and went on to suggest that since "many illusions in a cartoon are created with an airbrush...the background artist must be highly skilled in airbrush technique."

Indeed, it is the rare animated film, whether feature-length or a television commercial, that does not rely on the airbrush at the very least for backgrounds. Thus it was that the airbrush, in its first popular hour, was discovered for yet another use.

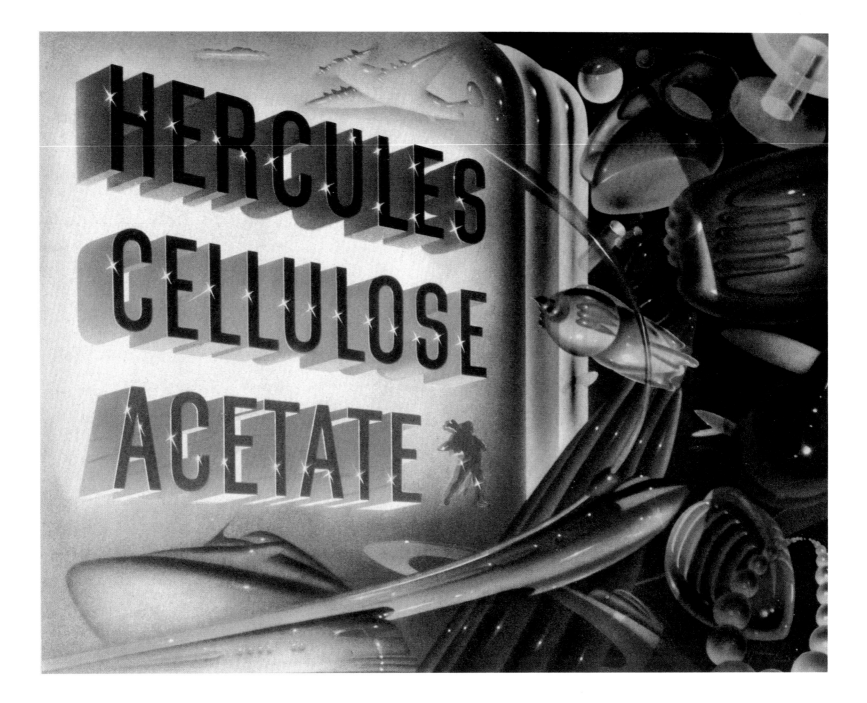

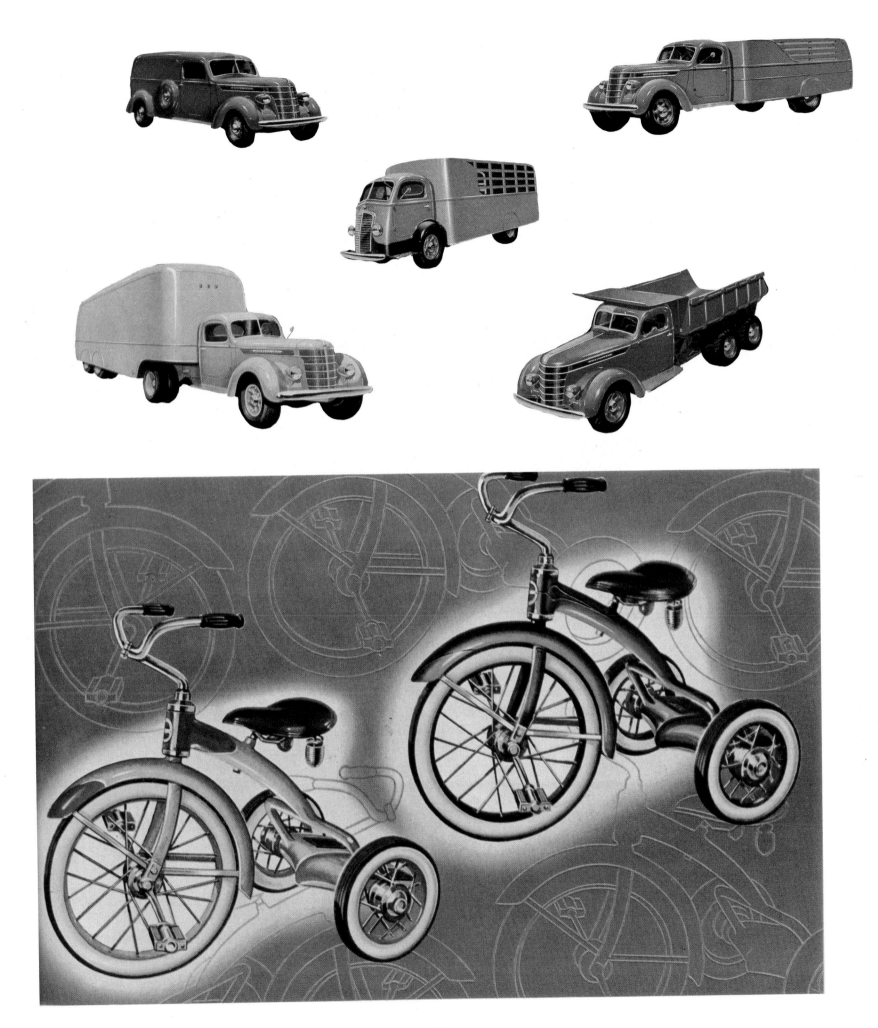

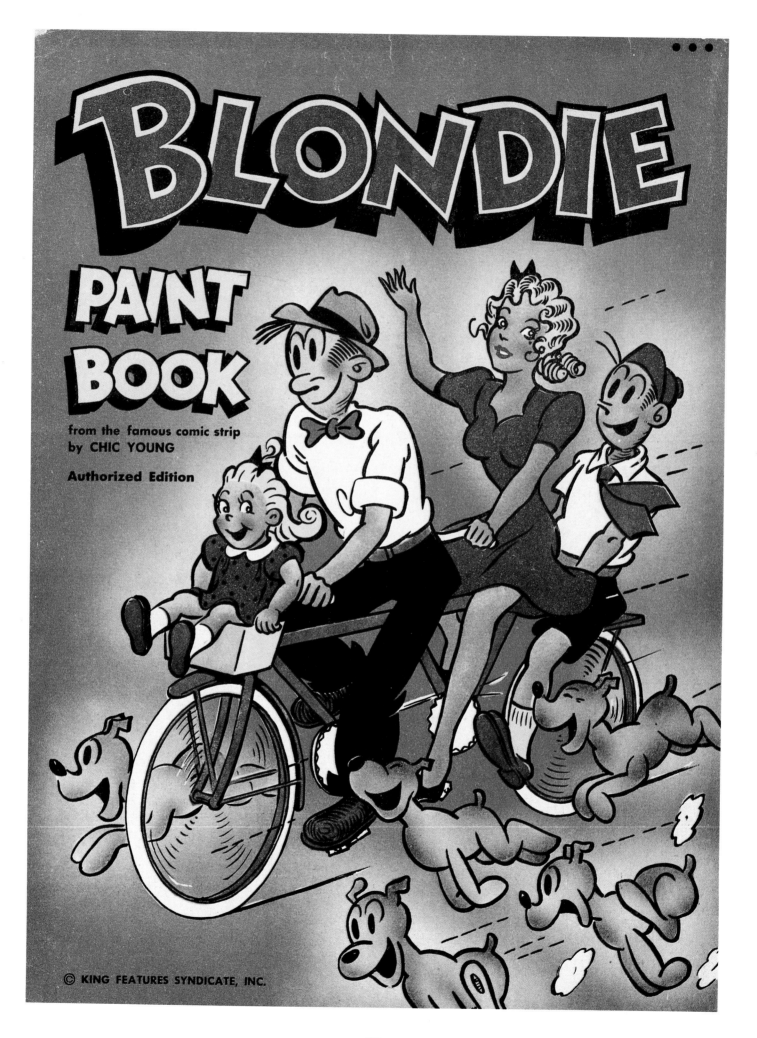

Otis Shepard 1945

Otis Shepard 1945

Dorothy Shepard 1936

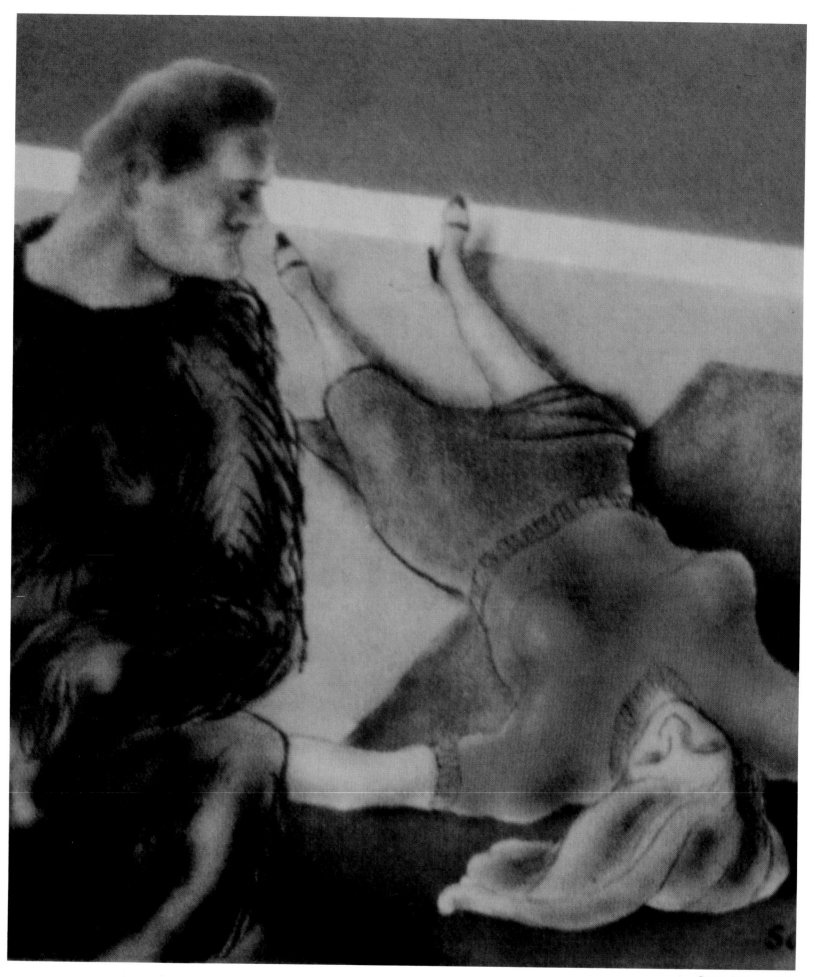

George Salter   1945

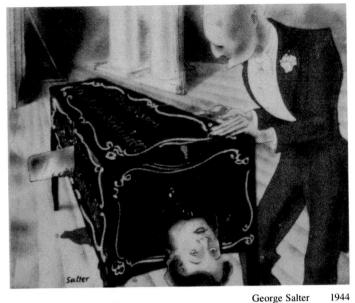

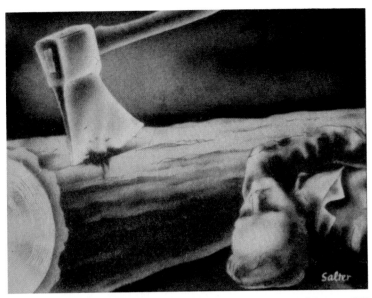

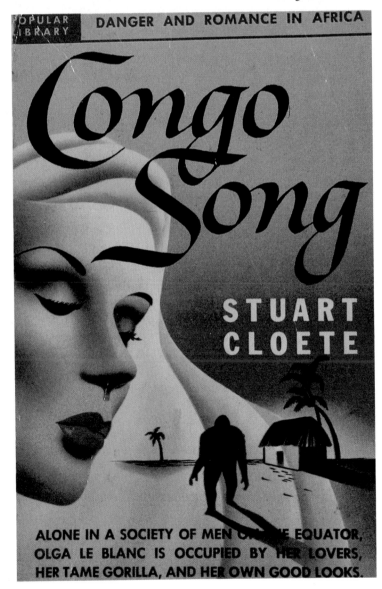

Night View of Lagoon of Nations, New York World's Fair

"WAY OUT WEST IN OLD WYOMING ACROSS THE HILLS AND PRAIRIES ROAMING"

Greetings From CHICAGO ILLINOIS

GENERAL MOTORS

THE STATUE OF LIBERTY AT SUNRISE, NEW YORK CITY

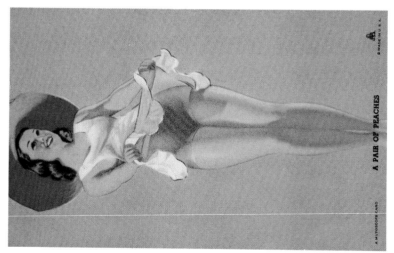

A PAIR OF PEACHES

FADE-OUT IN THE FORTIES AND FIFTIES   Until the revival in the late sixties, book covers commissioned by Dell Popular Library and the Mercury Mystery series were the last concentrated body of airbrush art. So prominent had the look been during the Depression and World War II that it became associated with those troubled years. Though airbrush work did show up in various ads and technical illustrations during the late forties and throughout the fifties, it was for the most part abandoned in favor of the paintbrush and the camera.

Initially used only for protection, book covers were finally recognized as an important factor in selling a book, and became, so to speak, the book's publicity agent.

George Salter was in large part responsible for the new approach to book jackets. As with all promotion, the inclination was toward strong, clear images, which Salter executed with great flair; his designs have a spontaneous appearance that is difficult to achieve with the laborious airbrush procedure. Of these covers, an article in *Gebrauchsgraphik* remarked: "They represent the decisive moment in book advertising, and the sales reports of the publishers go to prove that they are a very efficient form of propaganda."

After the spate of Salter book covers, the airbrush faded from use. But when it returned to popularity in the sixties, it was in conjunction with a different kind of cover —the record album cover.

INDIAN CHIEF

INDIAN RIVER FRUIT

PRODUCE OF U.S.A.

SHILOH FRUIT PACKING CO.
SHILOH, FLORIDA

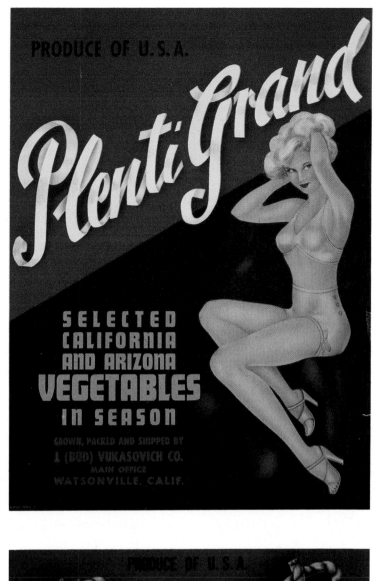

PRODUCE OF U.S.A.

Plenti Grand

SELECTED CALIFORNIA AND ARIZONA VEGETABLES IN SEASON

GROWN, PACKED AND SHIPPED BY
J. (BUD) VUKASOVICH CO.
MAIN OFFICE
WATSONVILLE, CALIF.

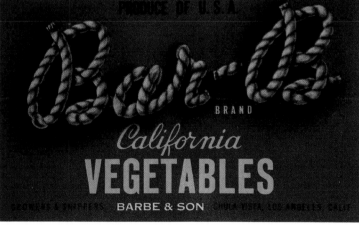

PRODUCE OF U.S.A.

Bar-B BRAND

California VEGETABLES

GROWERS & SHIPPERS   BARBE & SON   CHULA VISTA, LOS ANGELES, CALIF.

ROCK 'N ROLL   In the early sixties, the generation often referred to as the ''baby boom'' extended its collective arm to signal a halt: the almighty car, among other symbols of economic prosperity, was causing more fumes than fun, and economic prosperity extended its privileges only to certain classes within the Great Society. The sixties generation had been reared with all the modern conveniences and didn't want them anymore. As is inevitable in a profit-driven society, this attitude itself became marketable.

Posters, which had suffered a decline from the late forties through the fifties, came back full force to advertise rebellion. And photographic realism, which had dominated advertising art in the previous decade, was replaced by fanciful illustration. Just as the airbrush had emerged as a popular medium after its frequent retouching use in the twenties, so did it once again come in on the heels of photography. Social unrest was not only something you could buy and hang on your wall; with the Beatles, rock 'n roll combined the pulsating rhythms of rock with the quality of folk lyrics and was soon established as a major industry: social unrest became something you could dance to.

Alan Aldridge   1973

Robert Grossman   1967

Robert Grossman

Robert Grossman   1970

In England in 1963, this new sound was matched by an equally adventurous look in advertising art. This visual revolt was led by *Alan Aldridge*. In contrast to the geometric shapes of Cubism that had predominated for almost a half-century, Aldridge's airbrush illustration was lavish and rounded, reminiscent of Art Nouveau. The airbrush was back, and this time would demonstrate all of its extraordinary versatility. Particularly adept at highlighting, Aldridge created images that leapt out at the viewer; indeed, in preparation for much of his work he is known to erect three-dimensional models. In addition to numerous illustrations, Aldridge has produced a television cartoon series, and he edited a book of lyrics by the Beatles, with whom he shared a small revolution.

In America, such innovators as *John Van Hamersveld, Robert Grossman, Dave Willardson* and *Bob Zoell* were also picking up the airbrush as they changed the look of illustration. Zoell can't remember what inspired him to experiment with the airbrush in 1967. He had first used the instrument in the fifties, when his father presented him with one as a gift, but he hadn't even thought about it for a number of years. It is likely that his frustration with the Los Angeles graphics company for which he worked encouraged Zoell to ''start cooking'' with the airbrush. His illustrations, and those of Grossman and Willardson, caught the eye of *West*'s art director, Mike Salisbury, and the revival of airbrush art was at hand.

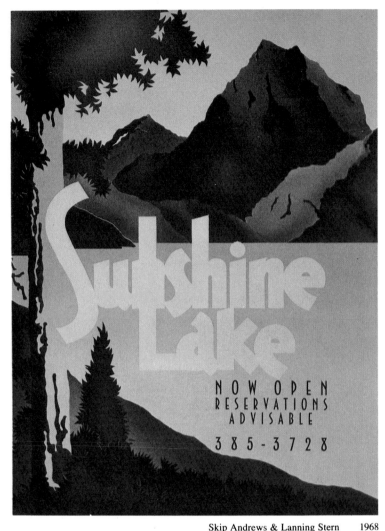

Skip Andrews & Lanning Stern   1968

Lanning Stern   1969

Lanning Stern, a designer and champion of airbrushing, underscores the importance of Salisbury's contribution, noting that older art directors were resisting the airbrush look on the grounds that it was dated and, even worse, filled with bad memories. For Stern, who was actively interested in thirties graphics and, particularly, the work of Joseph Binder, Zoell's imagery in *West* announced a kindred spirit. He contacted Zoell and they, along with Willardson, *Tim Clark, Skip Andrews,* and *Ed* and *Frank Mel* produced hundreds of airbrushed magazine ads, album covers and illustrations. As was their intention, this airbrush outpouring initiated a bona-fide revival. Ria Lewerke, an art director who does a lot of work in the music industry, explains the phenomenon: ''The airbrush is California. It's rock 'n roll.''

Lanning Stern 1969

Skip Andrews & Lanning Stern   1970

Skip Andrews & Ed Mel   1970

Though dismissed by some members of the art world as a superficial—hence, to them a uniquely California—style, the airbrush is, in fact, capable of heady wit and informed commentary. Zoell himself derived a great deal of pleasure from the cartoon characters he became known for. He particularly enjoyed the fact that these little creatures, by mere virtue of their presence in an advertisement, poked fun at the very products they were supposed to be promoting. And when the biting caricatures of Robert Grossman began to appear in *New York, Time* and *Newsweek,* they were immediately celebrated by artists and intellectuals alike. Pete Hamill, for example, described them as having "the subtle power to change the way we perceive reality. Once you see one of his airbrushed caricatures of a national politician, it is impossible to see that politician in precisely the same way again."

Skip Andrews & Ed Mel   1969

83

In the hands of Zoell, Stern, Grossman, and Willardson, the airbrush regained its stature as a valuable medium. And with the unorthodox contributions of *Charles White III* and *Doug Johnson,* advertising art got hip. Whether earthbound or mystical, the humorous and inventive work of these artists renders any distinction between applied and fine arts increasingly tenuous. In the seventies, the airbrushed illustrations of *Peter Lloyd, Peter Palombi, Philip Castle, Hans Ulrich* and *Ute Osterwalder,* and *Roger Huyssen* can certainly be considered a contemporary art form. In fact, the airbrush has enjoyed so much popularity during the decade that there are some who have suggested its future designation as the art form of the seventies.

Frank Mel   1970

John Van Hamersveld   1977

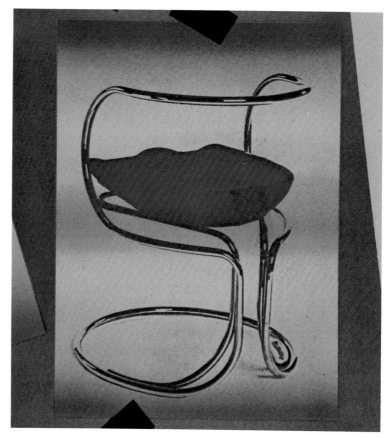

John Van Hamersveld   1977

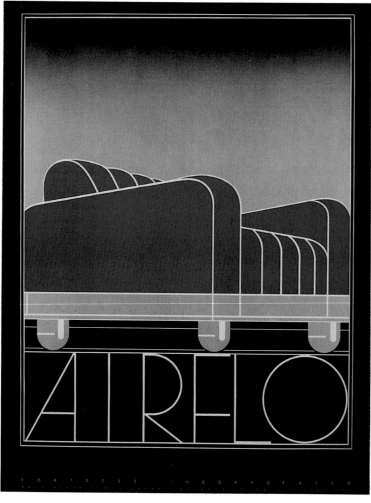

John Van Hamersveld   1976

John Van Hamersveld   1973

John Van Hamersveld   1976

Gary Panter   1979

The airbrush, however, has not stagnated, nor is it
likely to. In the Dadaistic iconoclasm of *Mick Haggerty*
and *Gary Panter* and the photographic experimentation of
Taki Ono, it shows every sign of remaining with us as a
volatile instrument that will continue in the full range of its
remarkable art to reflect the fluid attitudes of society.

   ''Aesthetic environments raise our ethic consciousness—art is the measure of the consciousness and culture
of a nation. The visual impressions of advertising have the
greatest influence on taste and culture as they far out-
number the impressions received from museums and art
galleries.''   *Joseph Binder*

Portfolios

Alberto Vargas

argas. To many, the name is synonymous with female sensuality, a generic term whose meaning is unmistakably one with the style, grace and beauty of the American woman. Spanning a half-century of changing ideals—from the Ziegfeld Girl to the Playboy Bunny—a creation called the Vargas Girl has somehow managed to captivate the fantasies of a nation. This enduring achievement would seem unlikely. But among those very few things that can truly be considered universal, there is the passionate love between a man and a woman. The Vargas Girl was born of such a love.

In his modest home in suburban Los Angeles, the native Peruvian tells the story. His accented voice rises and falls with each remembrance, but the lyrical tone is constant. Soon the listener experiences the presence of a profound emotion, an emotion so strong that it cannot help but add a new dimension to the appreciation of human sexuality and the art that derives from it.

In 1916, Joaquin Alberto Vargas y Chavez decided to postpone his further study of art in war-torn Europe. In order to return to Peru, he would have to sail via the United States. "When I landed in New York, I took one look and knew it was 'Goodbye, Dad. I'm sorry—I'm not coming home.'" The pace, excitement, and most of all, the "torrent of girls" immediately established New York as a new home for Vargas—he had found his artistic milieu. It was the Jazz Age, a time of flappers and fashion when a young man with a good eye for both could find work— even an immigrant with few connections. Alberto worked at first retouching negatives and drawing hats, all the while developing his skill in watercolor, oil and pastels. He was by this time committed to a career in art, and this belief sustained him. Within two years he made his first freelance sale. And he met Anna Mae Clift. "When she appeared on the scene, I knew here was something I had never seen before. She had natural red hair, and the palest blue eyes that you can think of. There were many Southern girls in New York, but not one like her."

The daughter of divorced and impoverished parents, Anna Mae had come to New York from rural Tennessee. A remarkably beautiful girl with intelligence to match, she became a favored show girl in the *Greenwich Village Follies*. To supplement her income, she modeled in Seventh Avenue's Garment District, and it was there that she met a sweet, unassuming painter. She was so taken with the manner and talent of the "little artist" that she not only agreed to pose for him, but also refused payment.

Anna Mae had left home in search of security, both financial and emotional. The little artist provided neither. Nor did she conform to his Old World standards of propriety. Though Alberto was undeniably mesmerized by Anna Mae, her active participation in the big city's night life met with his staunch disapproval. Further hindered by a language barrier, their relationship was for years restricted to that of artist and model, both stubbornly resisting the growing personal attachment that each felt for the other.

One fact, however, was acknowledged: in Anna Mae, Vargas had found the perfect American woman. His struggle to capture that perfection on paper was to become his life's ambition. And from the start, his work reflected this great discovery. The soft tones he began to achieve with watercolor, combined with his distinctive facility with the airbrush, gave his female figures unique and unprecedented allure. And this new look soon attracted the shrewd attention of Florenz Ziegfeld, whose handshake launched the career of Alberto Vargas. For nearly ten years Vargas executed the official portraits of the Ziegfeld court, and he credits the master showman with having taught him "the delicate borderline between a nude picture, and a nude with style and class."

The "little artist" now had a different stature. He could offer Anna Mae at least part of the stability she so desperately needed. But his luck, as that of all artists, could easily reverse. Anna Mae would not yet succumb to his charms, though she would, of course, continue to pose for him. Then, after nine years of working with her, the humble and gentle painter gathered all his courage and proposed marriage. Suddenly the truth was inescapable. He

laughs, recalling the moment. "She looked at me and said, 'I've been waiting all these years for you to open your mouth and say something.'"

The same iron will that had maintained their lengthy emotional distance would characterize the strength of their union. Two singularly forceful people became forever committed to the love affair that was their marriage. It kept them going through the Depression and the subsequent fall of the *Ziegfeld Follies*. It gave them the spirit to travel West to try their luck in Hollywood. There, with his inspiration at his side, Vargas found an incomparable environment for pursuing his goal of immortalizing the American woman. He worked at all the major studios, painting portraits of a parade of beauties the likes of which the world has not seen before or since. The Movie Star in the thirties—the glory days of Hollywood—was a natural for the hand and heart of Alberto Vargas. A natural, too, in any other relationship, for at least a little wifely jealousy. But Anna Mae, whose image was her husband's vision of sensuality, had neither the inclination nor the cause to feel jealous. It was not only her encouragement but her simple presence that fed his work. "She was an expert at easing me into what I was dreaming."

A necessary aspect of dreaming is the occasional rude awakening, the first of which occurred when his participation in a union walkout left Vargas unemployed. The studio doors slammed shut. As devastating as this was to their peaceful existence, it was a mere bout of fitfulness compared to the nightmare that followed.

The Vargas' moved to Chicago, where Alberto signed a contract with *Esquire*. That seemed at first a solution to their financial worries. After months of spotty advertising assignments, the magazine represented a steady and reliable market for the artist's work. Indeed, the Varga Girl (the *s* was dropped by *Esquire*) fast became a household term; pinups and calendars bearing her face and form gave enlisted men something to smile about during the otherwise bleak days of World War II. Vargas was working night and day to produce, under deadline pressure, the demanding number of portraits his new employer expected of him. Ever Old Worldly—he had started his career with a handshake—Vargas was oblivious to the preposterous contract he had signed as more or less an afterthought. When he complained to his publisher about the outrageous schedule he faced, Alberto was treated with disdain and accused of going back on his word. Once Anna Mae read

the contract, the hopelessness of their situation became apparent. The "little artist" was committed to a *minimum* of one painting per week for ten years! Moreover, he had signed away the Varga Girl herself; she was legally wedded to *Esquire*.

Vargas trembles with the pain of that unforgettable humiliation. "I felt as though my soul had been ripped from my body and stepped on." The image that he had created, the image that bore his name, did not belong to him. But the devotion of Anna Mae did. She refused to accept this defeat, nor would she allow her husband to accept it. Feeling utterly beaten, Vargas had told his wife that there was no choice but to fulfill his ten-year obligation to *Esquire*. She exploded. "I don't think I've ever seen her more furious than at that moment. Her eyes were just like two blue stars focused on me when she said, 'What are you saying? We are going to fight this to the very end!'" Anna Mae's powerfully stated arguments in court were instrumental in winning the case for her husband. That his work was also her work was never more clearly demonstrated than during the *Esquire* crisis. But the favorable verdict was appealed, then overthrown.

For a while it seemed that all was lost. How could a man's art be legally declared the property of someone else? To those fluent in the world of suits and countersuits, it is a notion that can be understood; to the agonizing artist, it was an unfathomable technicality. With nothing but their loyalty to each other and to their dreams, the Vargas' left the Chicago headquarters of *Esquire* and returned to their home in Westwood, California. Once again, the scramble for work and a life of hustling and hardship.

The Varga Girl was dead. But a close relation, and the true child of the Vargas' love affair was just then being born. In 1956 the Vargas Girl came to the attention of Hugh Hefner and effectively became immortal. To the millions of boys and men whose sexuality was awakened and aroused by the Vargas Girl's seductive glance in issue after issue of *Playboy,* the man who created her could only be a playboy of the highest order. But if a woman named Anna Mae had not remained by Alberto's side as both lover and wife, his faith in the perfection of feminine sensuality could not have been sustained; it was one woman, not many, who kept the dream alive.

Having found perfection in his heart, Alberto Vargas still seeks it in his work. When Anna Mae died in 1974, he says, "everything died with her." The passionate man stops talking, the loss shows in his eyes, his voice breaks. Then he continues, "I have had a wonderful life. I have learned a lot. . . . She was right, I cannot stop. There is in me at least ten more years of intensive drawing. The work I am going to do from now on is dedicated to her memory."

Bob Zoell

Zoell had it all: success and respect in his field, a house in the valley, a cocker spaniel curled up by the fireplace, and three kids asking Mummy where babies come from. Bob Zoell found the American Dream and then decided that he didn't want it anymore. Which is difficult to explain, but he is, after all, from Canada.

The son of a printer, Zoell grew up poor on the outskirts of Regina, Saskatchewan. He also grew up with the knowledge that he would be an artist. "From the age of three, my aunts, mother, everybody said how nice I could draw, and I grabbed on to that. (Obviously, I didn't scribble any better than any other three-year-old.) Even in Grade One, I was acknowledged as a good artist. Except this one kid, Ralph, he could draw a lot better than me." Zoell, madman and family man, bridge-burner and systematic planner, tells his story the way he makes his art—with irreverence and precision, mockery and earnestness. A man of a million contradictions, he's just the guy to do those wacky cartoons with an airbrush.

Ralph notwithstanding, Zoell's ability to draw (specifically, to copy pictures of Jesus) got him through an otherwise tedious career in parochial schools—that ability and a knack for dodging the bothersome dogma that is the

hallmark of Catholic education. "I didn't take any of that stuff seriously. At Communion they told us, 'If you let the Host touch your teeth, it's a venial sin. If you bite it, you're gonna go to hell!' " Zoell, no fool, made sure that the Host passed clear of his teeth, taking it right on the tongue; his time to tempt fate would come later. But it is with an immediate and acute sense of injustice that he recalls, "So you got this thing on your tongue and you're hoping it won't touch your teeth and you're just this little guy . . . and then the priest, of course, got the wine!"

A further lesson in life's injustices presaged Bob's disillusionment with commercial art. His older brother, sharing the family's pride in the young artist and being of an enterprising nature, decided that those copied pictures of Jesus had definite commercial potential. At age ten, Bob watched his first paintings roll off his father's printing press and into the marketplace. His brother's door-to-door pitch yielded a sale at the not unimpressive price of $10, of which Bob saw not so much as a nickle. But he did see that his art was a reasonable ticket to an independent (and non-Catholic) future.

With that lesson in mind, he quit school in the tenth grade. A series of jobs, from sign printing to engraving, provided a practical, paid education and the chance to develop a variety of skills. During this period, two events combined to push Zoell in the right direction: his father gave him an airbrush for Christmas, and he met Mary Fedak. "When I was seventeen, I airbrushed three Valentines for her. Instead of hanging them up, she put them in her hope chest, which really got me mad. After about a

month I got some white paint and brushed my name off them." What the dispute gained in intensity it lost in endurance, and in the end did nothing to forestall their marriage. Nor did it discourage Bob from pursuing the airbrush and a career in art.

When some of his friends said they were going to Los Angeles, he didn't hesitate. Though ambitious, his fantasies had taken him only as far as Vancouver; finding work in L.A. was enough of a long shot to be worth a try. After the requisite number of rejections, some from art directors who later would eagerly seek him out, the kid from the backwoods of Canada who knew he could draw was employed as a commercial designer. "I got a job right on the Strip; it was really a trip for me. People calling each other 'Baby,' and everything." Visa and family followed, with the American Dream not far behind. While ultimately more lucrative than creative, a steady job with a growing design studio is what houses in the San Fernando Valley are made of. This much Zoell already had, so the family moved into the perfectly charming Tudor that was complete with everything but picket fence (which Bob added years later, once he decided to sell).

He could tolerate the increasingly managerial aspects of his job only for so long. Bob wanted to experiment with ideas rather than fulfill commercial expectations. To that end, he left his job and opened a studio with his friend Doug Carr. They did well, designing packages and promotional materials for major toy accounts, flourishing in the booming market of mid-sixties advertising. But Saul Bass's organization, a respected leader in graphic design,

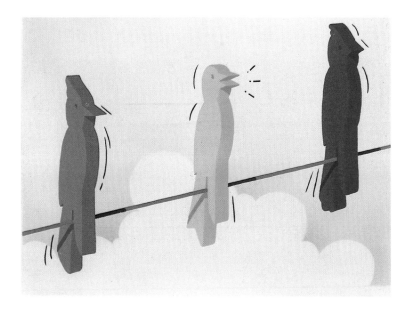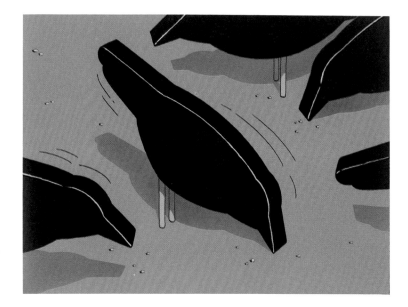

lured Zoell back into the company fold by offering him the position of Art Director/Supervisor in Corporate Identity and Packaging. It was a big title and a big year for Bob, who could endure the tedious paper work in exchange for the contact with Saul Bass. "It was worth it," he remembers. "I got to attend meetings with him and I learned a lot about things, like the psychology of sales." The psyche of Bob Zoell, meanwhile, was leaning toward images best not brought up at a sales meeting. Defining it as "an intuitive thing," he was becoming increasingly fascinated by whimsy and cartoon. There was no question about it—he had to get out of the corporate structure and work on his own.

At about time, Roland Young at Capitol Records, Mike Salisbury at *West,* and Jean Paul Goude at *Esquire* enlisted as enthusiastic supporters of his airbrush work, and Zoell became very hot. Indeed, he could buy more logs than he could burn in the fireplace at home. Word of his versatile airbrush style spread rapidly among his peers; and artists like Charles White III went from interest to curiosity to belief. In fact, there are few contemporary airbrush artists who do not acknowledge Zoell as a major influence. With requests for album jackets and magazine covers pouring in, Zoell hit his stride and crossed the line from making a living to making money. He had arrived in a big way, life was sweet, and dreams of fame and recognition were realized in the bright light of day. "I was mainlining bunny rabbits. I really got hooked on those little characters."

But "Handling notoriety and doing good work at the same time is very difficult. You become known for something, and then that's all they want." It was not long before Zoell wanted out—out of "commercial bean selling" and cartoon characters. The man had O.D.'d on bunny rabbits. In 1970 he stopped airbrushing. His clients wouldn't bend, and he started losing them. Not to worry: there was plenty of money in the bank, and the occasional ad he did accept brought him top dollar. Determined to paint his way to fame, he rented a new studio and allowed himself two years. "When you go into fine art, there's no other way to go in but naïve." Three years and thousands of dollars later, he had to give up the studio and convert his garage; it was bank-loan time. Then two more years of frenzied explorations into art. Why red? Why blue? Why red with blue? Why not blue with red?

When he stopped long enough to have a look around him, the scene at home posed sterner questions. For the sake of art, he had been willing to forgo the American Dream; now it seemed that he had sacrificed his family as well. The comforting fireplace tableau was shattered, and Zoell could only wonder, "Why art?" His passion had become his nemesis and he could recoup his losses only by rejecting art in favor of his love for his wife and children. Together, the family decided that they should leave the frantic pace of Los Angeles. Bob built a picket fence and sold the house.

As we started to put this book together, Bob Zoell's name was mentioned repeatedly, but no one knew anything more specific about his whereabouts than that he was "up in Big Bear someplace." Big Bear, California, is eighty miles northeast of Los Angeles, in the Angeles Crest Mountains; the climate is clean and crisp. Big Bear is, in short, a good spot for two people from Canada who need to look again at themselves and each other. At first abrupt, the change gradually became acceptable to the Zoells, and the L.A. desperation receded. "Two years in the mountains," says Bob, "has allowed me to be myself."

Just before he "came down the hill" to return to Los Angeles, Bob summarized the enormous range of his recent and difficult contradictions in a piece called "In Between." The retreat to Big Bear was neither an escape nor a solution to the conflict and turmoil that sent him there along with his family, and "in between" is where Zoell places himself today. But the important thing is that some people cannot stop making art. And for now, that's resolution enough.

Zoell is back in town. His card:

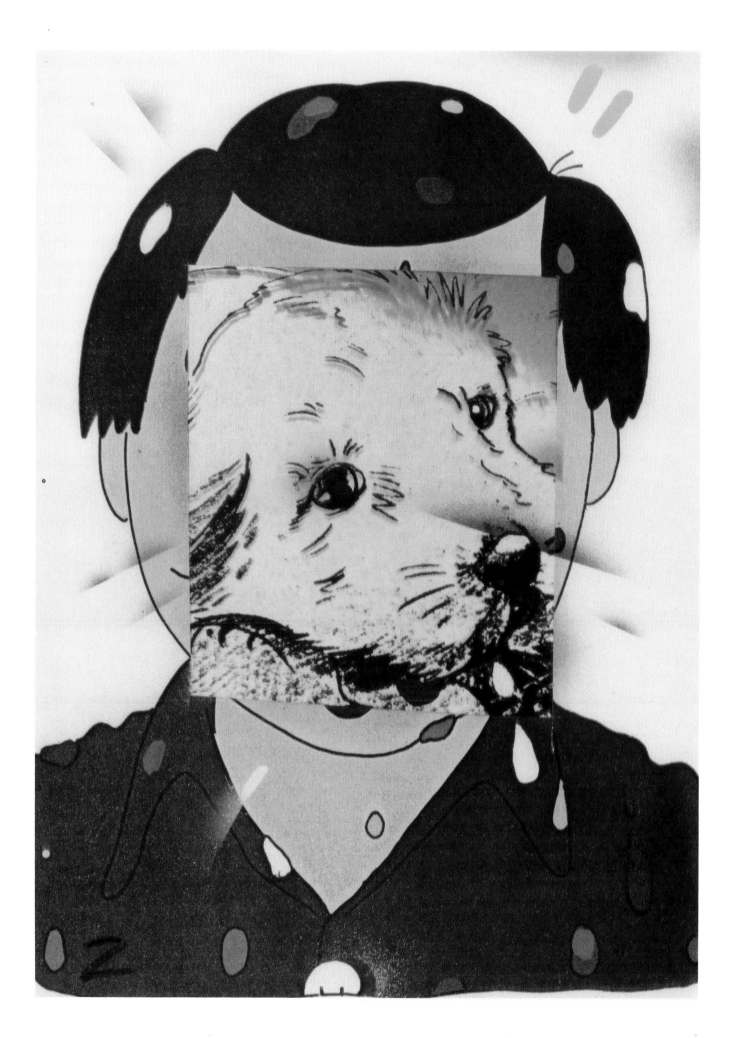

Charles White III

Charles White III is always into something new. He's done sculpture and watercolor, played with texture and perspective, staged happenings and sold T-shirts. And along the way he has become a master of airbrush illustration. His mother has a ready explanation: "He came out an artist."

A native of California, the kid who was "born with a pencil in his mouth" improved on nature by studying art and still believes strongly in the importance of knowing how to draw. But anyone familiar with Charlie White's work knows that copying an image is the furthest thing from his mind. Even if he repeats only himself, he considers it a ripoff. However thoroughly he has researched a job, whether he's working from a photograph or the object itself, interpretation is White's overriding concern. He may crack an egg on the floor and give it a long hard look, but his well-known painting of the egg on the floor for the cover of *Idea* magazine took form *after* he walked away from the actual egg, beat it around in his brain and blended it with his own distinctive vision.

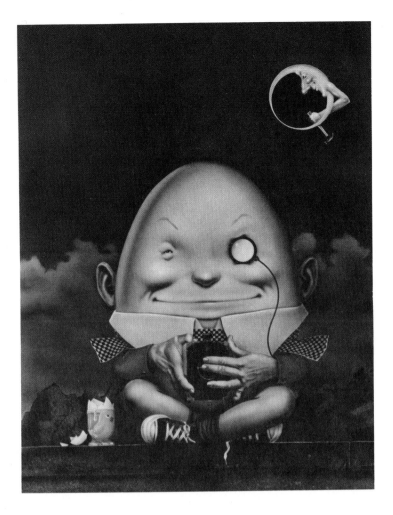

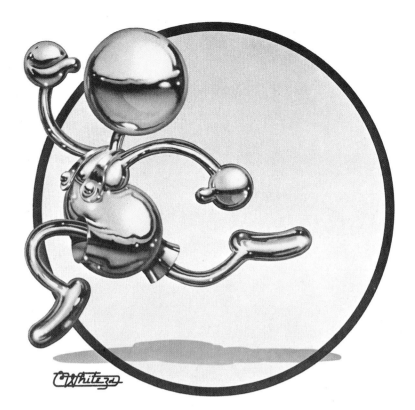

Broken eggs, cigarette butts in coffee cups, dented fenders, and flies—certainly an unusual array of subjects, and definitely among Charlie's favorites. "I like to paint things that people try to deny...things they don't like to look at. I used to call myself the garbage painter. I paint trash." People, of course, create trash, yet people are notably absent in his work. "It's not that I don't like painting people. But I'm more interested in showing a scene where a person *has been* or *will be*." Thus there is in much of his work a feeling of tension and expectancy, as well as a palpable energy that is also characteristic of White himself. It's not nervous energy but a strong sense of movement and fluidity that combines to create a promise of change.

A major change, for both Charlie and the world of illustration, came about in 1969 when he began to experiment with an airbrush. He was busier than he had ever been, turning out an enormous volume of work in the very precise medium of watercolor. One day he picked up the equally demanding airbrush, as much out of curiosity as anything else, and discovered that it was great for backgrounds. Then he saw that he could also make great circles and achieve myriad textures. An artist more than slightly inclined to try something new, White was immediately hooked. "The fascinating thing about airbrush is that you

you create these images without ever touching the paper. It's like magic." He soon moved from airbrushing backgrounds to the Lightcrust Doughboy, his first full-fledged airbrush piece.

Along with the medium came an attitude: "It was a way to express my new thinking. My work had been a lot more somber. All of a sudden I brought this happy stuff into my illustration." The new attitude was infectious, and as other artists followed his lead, Charlie naturally investigated still more innovative ideas. The tabletop series, with its play on perspective, was one of the first major accomplishments of his continuing, and highly successful, experimentation with the airbrush.

The greatest challenge for White is the very nature of his method. "It's a very laborious procedure, which is totally *not* my temperament." His business associate, Lynn Berman, concurs. "Charlie is gregarious, impatient, spontaneous. The airbrush is none of those things." On the other hand, and on more than one occasion, the quick-thinking artist has enjoyed explaining to an impatient art director that a job wasn't ready on time because "I ran out of air." Ironically, one deadline that Charlie feels he never met figures in one of his most famous pieces, the Screaming Yellow Zonkers poster. Given only two weeks for the job, he spent a full week executing the intricate drawing. By the time he picked up the airbrush (an instrument that he was not yet as fluent with as he came to be), day and night together didn't allow him to even approach his own

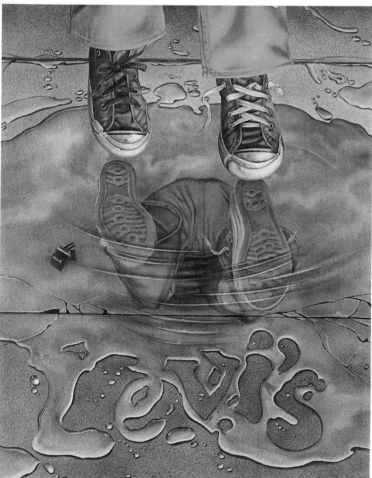

high standards. Working on two pieces, he found that it was extremely difficult to match the backgrounds, and he had to patch up the border several times. "When I got the proof back, I swore I'd never show it to anyone. I was so embarrassed by it. It still pisses me off that I never had a chance to finish that sucker."

Fortunately, Charlie derives more pleasure than pain from his work, and the fly that appears in about fifteen of his paintings is a fitting symbol for his unsurmountable levity. "I always try to sneak something of mine into every picture." The insect was hatched on an illustration for Talon zippers; quite spontaneously, as is his custom, he placed a fly on the donkey's head. The addition was his own little joke, and he never dreamed that the fly would survive to see print. That his employers shared his enjoyment brushed away what little hesitation White had for injecting his own ideas into an assignment.

The stream of ideas great and small that flows from Charlie White is unlikely to run dry for quite some time.

One of his larger ambitions is to design special effects for movies, a scheme he might well have conceived while doing the poster for *Star Wars*. This was a job he didn't really expect, since "Lucas didn't like airbrush. I don't know why they hired me." But they did, and he was suddenly sitting alone in the huge Academy Theater in Hollywood, watching in solitude the movie that would soon draw standing-room-only crowds. The poster (a collaboration with portrait artist Drew Struzan) reflects Charlie's vision of what he interpreted less as a fantasy of the future than as the ultimate swashbuckler—a timeless story of adventure.

Charlie's future plans for movies are finally a reflection of his own adventure. More than anything, it's challenge that he seeks, in his life as well as in his work. "I've always had this thing for the unreachable. That's why I want to get into film. It's something that I can't really reach. And that's what turns me on and makes me move." Given his track record on challenges, if Charles White III is moving, he'll get there.

Dave Willardson

ave Willardson is the kind of cowboy peculiar to the sixties generation: his feet are planted firmly on the ground and his head is off somewhere in space. An astute businessman, he knew since the seventh grade that he wanted to be a *commercial* artist. "There was no other answer. That was what was going to happen." Yet he's always been attracted by imaginary worlds. Hence, in 1960 he left college after one semester to take a job as a ride operator at Disneyland. "My desire to go to work there instead of continuing on at college might be indicative of how much I enjoy staying in that fantasy realm. And I didn't get there and find I was disappointed, because the magic really existed...still does."

But financial security beckoned, so he was off to the Los Angeles Art Center to work toward his goal of a successful reality. There he met a former Art Center student, Charlie White. "He saw my work and asked me to come over and help him with some things. We got along well, worked will together, and after about a year and a half of working with him, I started getting somewhat independent, picking up some of my own accounts."

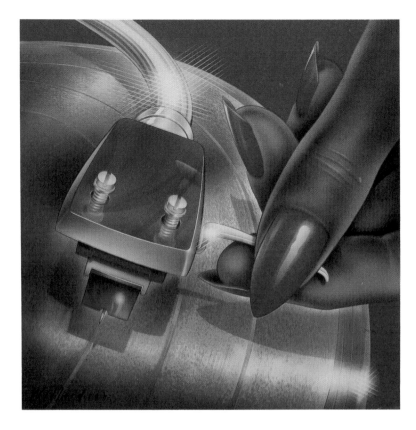

One night during his tenure at White's studio, Willardson sat puzzling over a problem he was having with an illustration. Like Bob Zoell, when he was a kid he had received an airbrush from his father; unlike Zoell, the memory of that gift prompted him to get his airbrush out of the drawer years after it had been given to him. "It was in 'sixty-five, one of my first [independent] illustrations. I was trying to gradate a color and I couldn't get it to grade. It looked crude and I kept trying and trying on this thing for two weeks. And I finally just figured out that if I could hook up that airbrush and get some color going through it, I could grade that color. It was a great solution to a struggle that had been going on for two weeks."

As far as Willardson knew, no one else in the country was using the airbrush at that time. He was, however, soon to learn of the very negative connotation the tool carried. "At the time, it was 'photo retouching' and really, really lame." Nevertheless, the airbrush worked for him, and he enjoyed using it. "I realized, when I sprayed that paint,

that I really had something." So sure was he of this exciting new method that he did several jobs for free, to ensure that the pieces would be printed; donation was the only way, because most of the art directors did not share his enthusiasm. "I showed my portfolio of about a dozen pieces and everybody put me down. They'd find out the stuff was done with airbrush and say, 'You mean you're a retouch guy?' That was the only point of reference anybody had for it." If they were reacting against a look that reminded them of the war years, they weren't saying so. And it wasn't until later that Willardson discovered the history of airbrushing. "We bring it back thirty years after it was really popular. It was so exciting to see all this beautiful chrome and forties things and know that airbrushing's the only way in the world they could have done it."

One art director, Mike Salisbury of *West* magazine, did like Willardson's work. "He saw some of my stuff, called me up and gave me thirteen jobs. It forced all the art

directors who looked in *West* to accept this technique. It was an endorsement"—one that led to popularity and, within a year, to an income that satisfied his business ambitions. And his fantasies were satisfied by the fact that he had found a technique with which to express his imaginative ideas. "The only way I could be happy working or painting was to have these fantasy things crop up in my work. What gave me the courage to realize that you could put this kind of thinking in your work was my being around Charlie White. He introduced a lot of silly, crazy sorts of things into jobs and realized you could get away with it. I was very young in the business, and he was a

good influence on me."

The compound satisfaction that Dave Willardson feels today derives, for the most part, from his early determination to stick with a medium that he knew was right, both for him and for illustration. Indeed, it is largely due to his conviction and inventiveness that airbrushing has become a major force in illustration.

"To see this thing take place was like mining for gold and then striking a vein and knowing that you've really struck! . . . If I have accomplished anything in my lifetime, in my entire career, one of the greatest things I have contributed was the night I hooked that airbrush up."

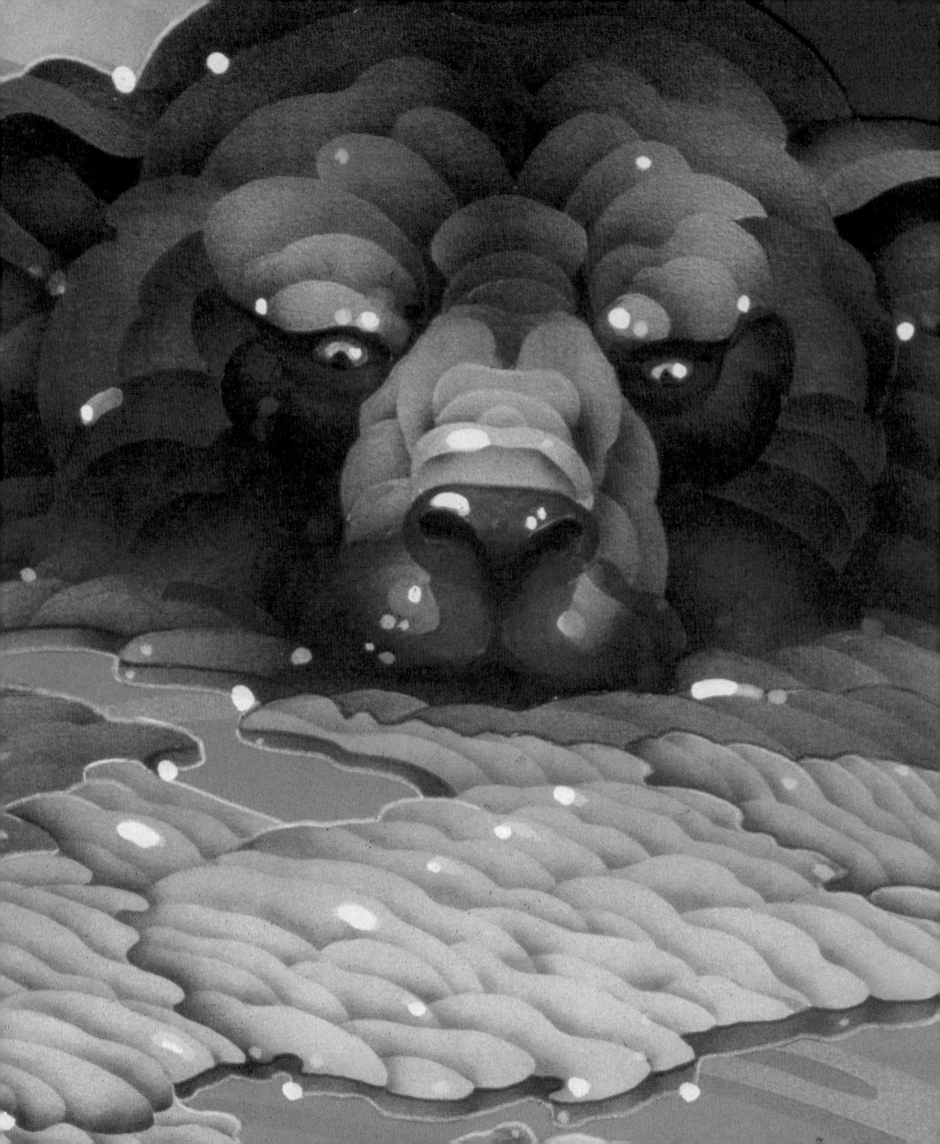

Doug Johnson

Doug Johnson was once asked to draw a straight line for a promotional spread in a trade publication, the idea being that several well-known illustrators would draw lines and get credits for their contributions. "I knew everyone else would take it seriously, so I just picked up my brush and did this," he explains with a zigzag gesture. "So it was all these straight lines with credits and then there was this"—again he makes a zigzag motion—"with my name next to it. More characteristic of my style, anyway."

Just as those flowing lines are representative of the artist, so are they representative of the man—his personality, his career and his goals. "Sometimes I'm glad that I'm an advertising consultant...then I just want to go off by myself and paint, sit quietly with no one talking at me... then I long to be in a meeting arguing concepts. It's really a back-and-forth kind of thing."

His success, which has not been a back-and-forth kind of thing, began quite appropriately in 1970, when Johnson decided to take some time off. Having come to New York from Toronto about a year earlier, he felt that he needed to get out of the city and into a more peaceful environment where he could develop his style. Just then the Society of Illustrators called to ask if he'd do the poster for their annual show. "Every art director, every ad agency, every illustrator in the country would see that poster. It was incredible!" So instead of becoming temporarily scarce, as he had planned, Doug Johnson became known to everyone in illustration. And within weeks, his work would come to the attention of not only illustrators, but the entire population of New York City. "Soon after doing the Society of Illustrators poster, I got this strange phone call from a guy with some kind of heavy accent," he remembers. "All I could

understand was that the guy was from the phone company, so I figured there was something wrong with my bill." When communication improved, Doug realized he was being asked to do a New York City Yellow Pages cover.

Johnson is known for his heavy use of highlights, a technique he first used on a series of illustrations for *Look* magazine, and which led to his football cover for *NFL* magazine. "When you watch football on television, there's always a kind of glare from the lights. I just formalized that, and it worked." This explanation makes Johnson's technique sound very spontaneous, but he claims that, "In fact, it's very planned out." Indeed, fine craftsmanship is required to successfully create the illusion of irresponsibility, and Johnson is above all a master of calculation.

Like Francis Bacon, whom he used to hate and has since acknowledged as a major influence on his work, Johnson establishes a flawless base, which he then dismantles, and in this he is unique among current illustrators. "When I started doing what I do, people were buying acrylics. It was a very cool, uninvolved kind of art; things looked totally untouched by human hands. So I got my underpainting of reality in there with the airbrush, and then messed it up. Like pavement graffiti, showing that a human being had been there." The result of this precise "underpainting" and controlled "messing up" is a voluptuous blend of brush strokes and light.

Aspiring commercial artists are fortunate that the articulate painter is also an enthusiastic teacher. At the School of Visual Arts and at Syracuse University, and as part of a New York lecture series at his alma mater, the Ontario College of Art, Johnson opens his classes by remarking, "If you have the right brush, you can paint exactly like your hero." After this tongue-in-cheek comment about technique, the soft-spoken artist goes on to explain, "I'm trying to de-emphasize the idea of technique and to stress the need for personal vision. I want to teach a way of thinking, as opposed to a way of working." He notes that the artist's

vision need not be frustrated by commercial illustration, and that one of the reasons he enjoys working with art directors is that they provide an outline, or frame of reference, into which he can inject his own interpretation.

When approaching an assignment, Johnson's cardinal rule is to look at his subject—be it a word, a person, or an object—as if he's never seen it before. "Growing up in Canada, we got a lot of English television and radio. A satirical radio program called *The Goon Show,* with Peter Sellers among others, was my favorite. It made *Monty Python* and *Saturday Night Live* look mild in comparison. The bizarre humor of it taught me how to see things from a lot of different angles." Johnson's approach to a *Skeptic* cover story on improving U.S.-Cuba relations illustrates his point. Ever alert to the "different angles" of a subject, his seemingly light-hearted pairing of Uncle Sam and the Latin Lady makes for an arresting image of national personalities. "I like theatrics, a frontal assault. I want to grab the viewers' interest by catching their eye and then forcing it around in circles. Make them investigate and wonder. A lot of that comes from my training with art directors. Bring their eye back to the page after they've read that there's a sale."

Solitary painter and commercial artist, apparently spontaneous yet impeccably controlled, Doug Johnson isn't much interested in drawing straight lines. For him, meaning is less in the object itself than in the endless variety of ways one can see and depict the object. Summarizing this philosophy, he remarks, ''The whole point of art is that although it may not be functional, you can find a function for it in your life.''

He's serious for a moment, realizes the noncommittal —zigzag—nature of what he has just said . . . and then he laughs.

Peter Lloyd

eter Lloyd is quite frank about it: "The fact that I got into illustration is a total fluke." Following his interest in mass communication, he had enrolled in the Los Angeles Art Center in order to study automobile design; what, after all, has a greater popular appeal than the car? But shortly thereafter a funny thing happened: He won the Gold Medal from the Professional Society of Illustrators. (He no longer has this piece, done during his student days, having given it to his taxman one year when times were rough.)

Though he had never considered a career in illustration, Lloyd's head was understandably turned by this unexpected honor. In New York to accept the award, he began to wonder whether he could fit into the world of illustration. "I didn't see a clear niche for myself. It would be too easy to mimic other people." So after graduating from the Art Center (in the same class as future peers Dave Willardson and Dave Wilcox), he repaired to his native England to do some serious thinking about what to do next. Despite his apprehensions, Lloyd respected illustration as "art on a humane level. It communicates with people." Back in England, he wasn't communicating. As he told *Print* magazine, "When I was in England, I felt starved visually." Further, he felt cut off from a receptive mass audience. He has strong feelings about what he calls "the artist's vocabulary," which he defines as "how you see something." The elements of this vocabulary are form, color and the staging of subject matter—"It's how you see something, the texture you give life."

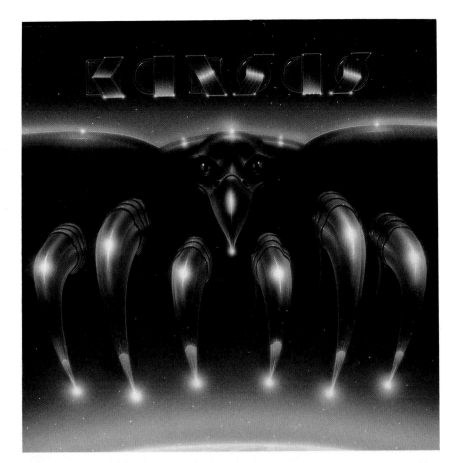

Lloyd was convinced that his impact could never be felt in England, and it was time for another Atlantic crossing. Returning to California, he found work but not satisfaction. Surrounded by such highly successful and close-knit illustrators as Bob Zoell, Lanning Stern and Charles White III, he felt like a student among masters—developing, but not yet in possession of, his own artistic style. The exposure to other styles, however, was helpful, and Lloyd picked up a great deal of information from Zoell and Stern, who visited his studio regularly.

Perhaps the most important thing he picked up was the airbrush that Stern left behind in his studio one day. Experimenting with it, Lloyd was excited to find that with this instrument he could achieve a look that was totally his own. Finally he could realize the ideas for art that he had entertained since arriving in Los Angeles—he had a vocabulary. ''I love to do something that looks totally untouched by human hands. I don't want bubbles or brush trails. Airbrush-applied pigment is perfect. It removes me from my art, turning everything into the way I see it, and it gives me total control.''

In 1975 his total control culminated in a cover for an album called *Atlantic Crossing*. The result was mass communication. Lloyd had heard and liked Rod Stewart's music. But the cover concept that was suggested by the art director was uncomfortably reminiscent of Doug Johnson's popular jacket for a record by Tina Turner. Clearly, the task at hand was to transform an already-used idea into a new package. Of course, Stewart was a man and Turner decidedly a woman, which was one step in the right direction. And having Stewart step across his cover in the right direction—namely, the opposite of that used by Turner to step across hers—was also an improvement. A horizontal image would mark yet another divergence from the vertical Johnson piece. Still, these were merely variations on a theme. What made *Atlantic Crossing* not only a great cover but also a landmark in Peter Lloyd's career was the success with which it communicated an abstract notion to a broad audience. Rod Stewart as master of a glitter-glamour world, that of seventies rock, is conveyed in every detail of this cover. That's what Lloyd saw, and whether or not the public consciously agreed, the image without doubt connected with something they, too, saw in Stewart. Thus it was this artistic Atlantic crossing that allowed Lloyd, after so many literal trips, to carry his vision to millions of people. He hasn't been out of work since.

His subject matter, which ranges from cocaine queens to toothpaste tubes, is alike only in that it entails a highly personal and emotional commitment, which is Lloyd's recognizable stamp. If he doesn't *feel* something for a subject, he won't even consider doing it; hatred is inspiration enough, but indifference is worthless. His favorite aspect of illustration is coming up with the idea; execution is secondary. And when an art director is at a loss for an album design or a magazine illustration, it's Peter Lloyd who is often called in. In fact, the concepts that he delivers are on occasion so compelling that more than one article has been retitled because of his illustration. "The Robots Are Coming" is one example of an article title that was inspired by Lloyd's interpretation of a manuscript. Recalling the thought process that went into the illustration, Lloyd says, "Robots vacuuming or cleaning your house, that's fun. But flying through space fucking, that's even more fun!"

These days Peter Lloyd is working on ideas that will require a few years of development and implementation. In the meantime his presence will continue to be felt on albums and in magazines. But Lloyd is a man whose desire to communicate is matched by ample talent, and before long, we will probably be able to see his ambitious gifts on display, say, in movie theaters across the country.

Peter Palombi

A A A A A A t thirty-one, Peter Palombi considers himself one of · the "next batch" of airbrush artists. In fact, although White and Willardson were major influences on Palombi, they rank his technique with the best.

The son of two art teachers, Palombi knew from the age of five that he would be an artist. His clear-sightedness did not meet with peer approval, and he was often the target of sneers and taunts. Still, he wanted to be an artist. With an Orange County background, he also wanted financial success. "I liked money too much to go into fine arts. I mean, fine arts was just silly. I pretended along the way that that was the direction, so I was a fine-arts major for three years at Chouinard, and then switched to illustration."

Having attended Chouinard College on a scholarship, Palombi is nevertheless grateful for the training he got in the fine-arts department. "It was fantastic. They taught us how to look at the things around us, how to view things." Enriched with this "conceptual maturity," he felt that he should then concentrate on technique. "Starting in high school, I was into drafting. I always admired precision." So he switched to the illustration lab. "In those days, Charlie White was like a god; I admired his work so much. I had no idea what kind of money was involved. All I knew was that just to be published would be incredible."

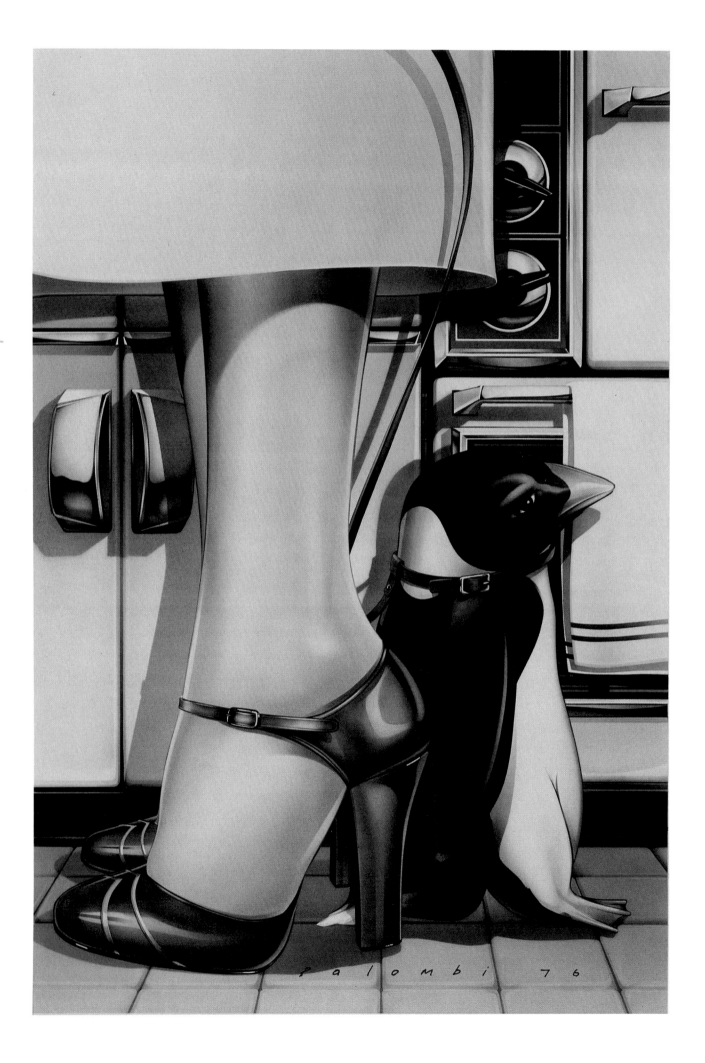

As an illustration student, Palombi was encouraged to make the rounds with his portfolio and was promised credits for any illustrations done professionally. "They had classes on how to price your work and how you should never leave an art director's office without a p.o. [purchase order]. They drilled that into us so much that when we finally got out and started showing our work, a lot of guys would say, if they were offered a job, 'Well, I'm not gonna do it until I get my p.o.' They were so adamant that it backfired, and the art director would say, 'Well, then, you can just buzz off.'" That never happened to Palombi. After he showed his book to nearly fifty advertising agencies in Los Angeles, the enterprising art directors at a well-known firm offered him the position of staff illustrator in a new company they were forming. Instead of a p.o., he got a 25 percent partnership in Rosenfeld, Wilson, Palombi and Dilts. "We got into full swing in 1970, and I left school. I learned a lot from them; I mean, those guys had been in the business. They were around forty, and I had just turned twenty-one."

The rigors of the commercial art world were not lost on the fledgling illustrator. Characteristically, he devoted himself to his work and put all of his energy into the career he had always wanted. "Once you get out of school and start working, every week is finals week for the rest of your life. You start to make promises to yourself and to your wife and children that this is going to be intense for the next five years, but after that it's gonna lighten up. And it just doesn't. You become like a fireman; you just put out fires. And they pay you well."

Simultaneously ingenuous and driven, Palombi doesn't do anything halfway. Having avoided the airbrush as being too trendy, when he finally bought one it was full steam ahead. He learned the basics from a book, feeling too embarrassed to go to Charlie White or Dave Willardson for help. "I never expected that I could have the technical ability. I had seen Vargas when I was growing up, and played with the airbrushes I could steal from my dad's drawer. But I just figured it was beyond me." Of course it wasn't, and after mastering the technique, Palombi

EDDIE HARRIS IS IT IN

Palombi '74

SD 1659

146

haunted old book stores, eager to discover all there was to know about airbrush art and artists. Yet his conscientious self-education also had its disadvantages. "I was into revival. All I was doing really was imitating other people and emulating their styles. But finally I had emulated so many styles that I ended up with my own. It was great. It's like somebody said, 'Hey, you got your own style!'"

Palombi defines his style as "choppy" and, like Doug Johnson's, "into shapes, but mine are bold square shapes. . . . I have to satisfy myself. The 'me' in the whole thing is really what is most important. I have no misconceived philosophies about providing good art for mankind." In his *personal* style, he is equally well defined. Free-lancing for the last several years, the "Shadow Man" (as he is often called by fellow illustrators) prefers mixing paints to mixing at parties, and is in fact something of a recluse. "When you're successful, people tend to flock. Stylish people that are maybe not in the business but in related businesses tend to become your friends. When they introduce you at a party, they don't say your name, they say what you are. If I go to a party and somebody asks me what I do, I say that I'm in the album recording business."

With his work as the driving force of his life, Palombi demands that it be challenging, that each new assignment

present a new set of problems for him to tackle and solve. "It's no fun to maintain. It's great to achieve. It's great to seek. It isn't exciting to do again what you've done before." He finds nothing so deadening as repeating something he's already done, and when he does accept this kind of job, he creates his own problems just to renew the challenge. "Graphically and aesthetically, if I have already solved the illustration they want, I see if I can do it in less time. If they give me two weeks, I wait until two nights before, to test myself and see if I can do it. . . . I know it's adolescent as hell."

Palombi's plans for the future suggest a more adult approach to sustaining his motivation. Intrigued with the theory that the less there is to look at, the more there is to see, Palombi is intent on exploring what he calls minimal art. "If you've got a table with people, maybe you eliminate the people, maybe you eliminate all of the settings and just deal with one place setting and the remnants of an event, something to symbolize what happened. That's where I'm going from here—to the place setting, to part of the place setting, to the spoon. The drag is that when I get into that spoon, I start doing the reflections and I get real carried away." He pauses. "Ah, I get into those reflections."

Roger Huyssen

hen you were young, you did things just for yourself. When you get old, you don't do those anymore. You start making money and you lose the greatest hobby of your life. It becomes a business." At the mythic age of thirty-two, Roger Huyssen is out of a hobby and into land-office business. On magazine covers, record albums, book jackets and movie posters, he has solidly established himself in the vanguard of illustration. And Huyssen is perhaps the first in a new breed of illustrator. As is not the case with other successful commercial artists, it was the method that gave Roger a career, rather than vice versa. "I would never have been an illustrator except for the airbrush. . . . Seeing it utilized in terms of advertising art was exciting. It made it fun for me to be an illustrator. Otherwise, I'd be something else."

Huyssen is also a member of an avant garde that envisions the removal of barriers between commercial and fine art. "There's a chance that it could happen in my lifetime. The images done on album covers have really been fine art in terms of attitude and the way they were executed. In relation to airbrush work, album cover art has become incredibly popular with the general public. The validity of illustration is that people see it."

Huyssen's background is indicative of someone for whom limiting definitions do not carry much weight. A native Californian who grew up on a surfboard, he majored in both fine arts and economics at the University of California at Santa Barbara and refuses to regard these pursuits as disparate. Nor, after serving in Vietnam, did Roger hesitate to consider a move from the West to the East Coast, an act often perceived as no less than a profound personal statement on the eternal dilemma of New York

154

versus Los Angeles. In a purely pragmatic fashion, he explains, ''Six months in New York is equal to two years in L.A. in terms of assignments and exposure, so in 1974 I moved.''

Though he found New York sufficiently hospitable to make his home there, Huyssen also found that many potential employers were bound by Coast-conscious prejudices. ''Originally, my work wasn't considered important. People

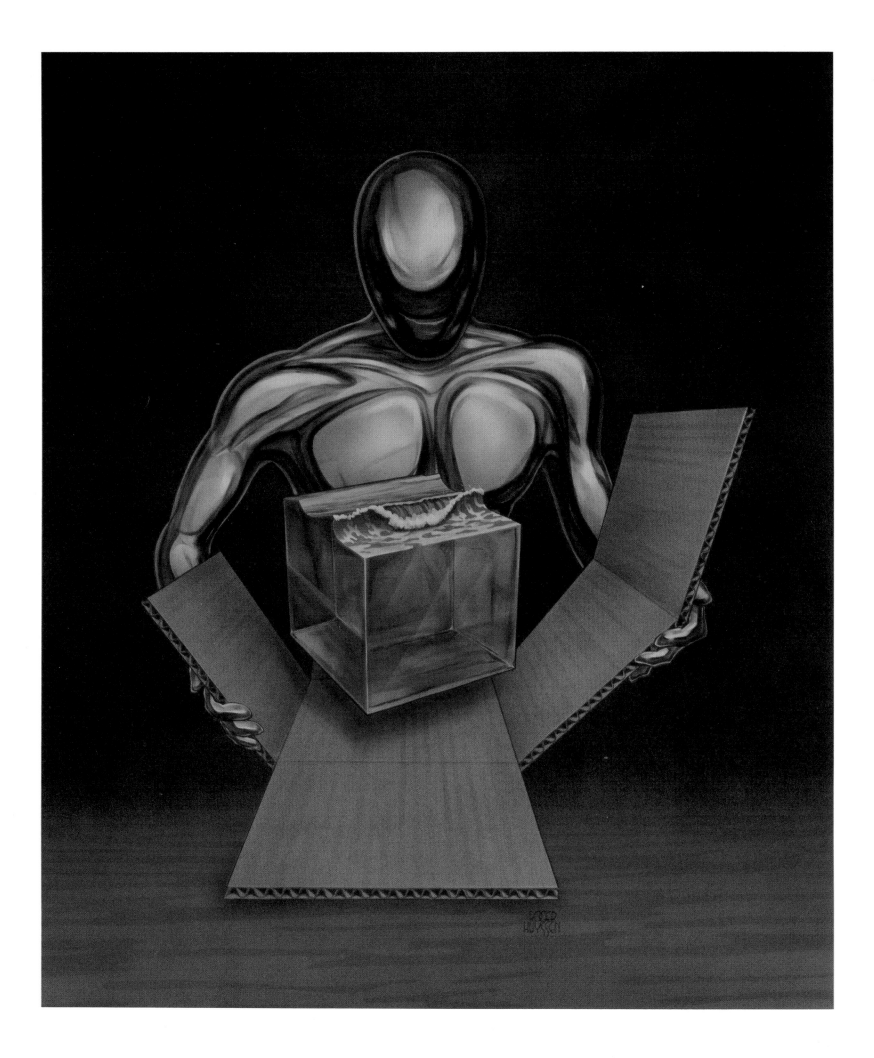

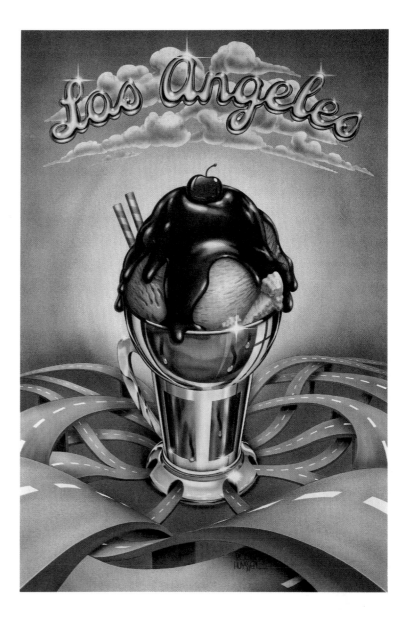

said it had a 'West Coast' look—good for the record business." To which Roger responded, "Well, there's lots of freedom in records," once again neatly side-stepping what might have been an insurmountable obstacle to a less flexible artist. Also, he knew that records offer visibility in addition to freedom, a combination that he has put to great advantage. One of his better-known pieces, the Jean-Pierre Rampal album cover, further tested his ability to deal with challenges. "When the cover was finished, I had the idea to put cigarette smoke coming out of the flute. You know, a cigarette after sex, and smoke rings coming out of a flute seemed like a natural. Rampal took offense because he had just quit smoking and was avidly opposed to it. We debated for weeks about whether to include the Surgeon General's warning on the cover..."

Although Huyssen firmly believes that "a record will sell because of what's on the grooves and not the artwork," he recognizes that the proliferation of his work in the music industry has certainly gone a long way toward selling *him*. Having parlayed the patronizing judgment of his illustration as "good for the record business" into "good for business—period," Huyssen now enjoys popularity with art directors in the advertising and publishing worlds who have come to appreciate the humor and inventiveness of his style. Indeed, it would seem that the "West Coast" look has an ever-broadening appeal.

Asked to name the major influences on his work, Huyssen replies in perfect Californian–cum–New Yorker style—at once ebullient and thoughtful. "Well, of course I love Charlie's work, and Palombi's. All of them, really. It's kind of incestuous; we all try to look different, but being connected is one of the great things about it."

Roger Huyssen is indeed a member in good standing of the "new breed." Though perhaps the only New York representative of the "West Coast" school, this singularity—to some perhaps a contradiction—suits him, for it is doubtful that Roger is concerned about anyone's attempts to categorize his art—or to define him, for that matter. As was impressed upon him with his American Manners piece for a *Time* cover story, one does well not to anticipate the future. "The first time they were going to print it, it had to be pulled because Pope Paul died. I had been told that it would definitely run the second time, barring World War III or the next pope dying. One hour later, I heard about John Paul on the news." The future course of Huyssen's illustration is equally unpredictable. As he says, "I'm always hot for anything new...no matter what it is."

Mick Haggerty

As a boy in England, Mick Haggerty carried his Sergeant Friday badge inside a little wallet, along with his identification card and bus pass. If not incredibly important to him, *Dragnet* was, he says, "something that I knew I liked quite well." And through the *Dragnet* books and programs, he learned about such places as Wilshire Boulevard and Benedict Canyon. One spring in England, while he was still in college, Haggerty and his girl friend were thinking about where to go on vacation; it seemed natural for him to suggest L.A. because "From *Dragnet* onwards, I always liked the idea of Los Angeles." He arrived in L.A. in 1973, and he's been there ever since.

Like many hopeful young artists in a new city, Haggerty spent a lot of his early L.A. days on the phone, trying to make contacts. "I was calling up all the art directors in town." He'd ask them if they would take a look at his book, and they'd tell him to drop it off. "I was getting the good old Secretary Waltz everywhere. It was very disheartening." But when John Van Hamersveld gave him Rod Dyer's number, his luck changed dramatically: not only did he get a job at Dyer's design studio, but on his first day of work, he got to meet all those art directors he had been calling.

In an act of hospitable friendship, Rod Dyer invited his new employee to have dinner with him at La Scala, one of L.A.'s priciest restaurants. After a quick stop at a clothing store, Haggerty picked up his girl friend, and they were on their way. "I dressed up and there we were. And at the table we see all these people I'd been trying to show my work to. I was going to have dinner with them! I can't thank Rod enough, because that was a really important thing." He stayed with Rod Dyer, Inc., for over a year, designing and illustrating record covers. And then he was ready to go out on his own. "Ever since leaving school, I like to do something different every two or three years. I *have* to do something different."

Haggerty's decidedly different style, heavily influenced by the unorthodoxy of Dadaism, met with favorable response from the commercial art world, and he was soon established as a free-lance illustrator. Rarely giving art directors what they had asked for, he nevertheless succeeded in giving them imagery that was arresting and communicative, making him a highly sought-after force in graphic illustration.

When, once again, the tireless experimenter began to look for a challenge, "something different," he bought himself an airbrush. The instrument, like everything else Haggerty approaches, was to be put to untraditional use. Even his colorful description of the tool defies all previously accepted definitions. "The airbrush is like a gun. In the hands of the amateur, it's a deadly weapon." Haggerty was no amateur, but his intentions with regard to

the airbrush were, and continue to be, strictly unprecedented. A confessed iconoclast, he readily discusses his perceptions of the tool. "A lot of people are fascinated by the airbrush because to use it well demands such dedication. It's rather like learning the guitar, like sitting down and figuring out the sort of technique Segovia uses. That's not the way I use it at all. To me, it's very much like a tool. And I use it for the things that other people are trying to avoid; I make it spackle and I make it spit and I put the wrong caps on. Sometimes I'll pick up an airbrush that's really cruddy underneath, and it'll be just fabulous for this one job I have. Then I just hope that whatever's in there doesn't clear out, or I'll lose those spackles."

What if a client requests a change in something he's done? He clears the air, if not his airbrush. "When someone asks me to repair a work that got damaged, I just have to start over. I can't pick up where I left off. My work is that casual. The other side of airbrushing is total control. There's no in between."

While some might consider his ideas shocking, L.A.'s Art Center has demonstrated its enthusiasm by seeking Haggerty's services as a part-time instructor. "It takes a lot of energy and time. A lot of commitment and no money. But it's fabulous," says Haggerty of teaching. "I want people to learn how to think rather than to learn a technique."

Despite, and because of, his totally original technique, Mick Haggerty has become a success story in the city of his childhood's favorite book. Working with a partner, designing special effects for films, he is excited by the possibilities of filmwork and collaboration. "I like to do some jobs totally on my own, to sit and see them come out of a blank piece of paper in a matter of hours. But there are other jobs where it's really nice to collaborate. You use a lot of creative and other judgments that aren't based solely on the canvas in front of you. You have to work on personality and timing, knowing what to say and who to use and how much further you can go. There's a whole adventure to it."

Taki Ono

Reminiscent of the earliest airbrush artists, Taki Ono's first ambition was to become an architect. But he had enrolled at Keio University, in Tokyo, as an economics major, and it was with that degree that he graduated in 1971. "Because of the difference of the educational system in Japan, once you started this major, it was very, very hard, almost impossible, to change. The first year I started, I was really going mad."

To allay his frustration, he took as many design courses as he could, and after graduating, came to the United States with the intention of studying architecture. Once arrived, however, he became intrigued with the Art Center in Los Angeles and decided to forgo architecture in favor of a career in commercial art. Enrolling at the Art Center, Taki Ono soon came under the influence of Mike Salisbury and Roland Young, two art directors who were central figures in the airbrush revival of the sixties. Though undeniably influenced by his native Japan, Taki also attributes an artistic impact to the United States, and particularly the West Coast. But Americana was not new to him: "Since I was born, I had so much influence from Western things, especially American things, because of my mother. She loved movies."

Airbrush technique was not part of the Art Center cur-
riculum. Aside from minor experimentation in Japan, Taki
didn't master this instrument until 1976. His first professional airbrush job was as a fingernail painter at a Beverly
Hills beauty salon. In need of employment and inspired by
the notion of airbrushing designs directly onto the fingernail, he was in the right city to find takers for the idea. Of
course he first had to go to beauty school. With his man-
icuring license in hand, so to speak, he spent several
months applying original airbrush designs onto the nails of
the fashion-conscious. But "after a while, I knew it was
impossible to keep doing this." During a year in Europe
and Japan he did a lot of camera work, and upon returning
to California, included photographs in the portfolio he was
putting together. At about this time he combined previous
experience with his new interest—by airbrushing over his
photographs—thereby creating the look for which he is
now well known.

The response from art directors was enthusiastic. Assignments came in from his former instructor, Roland Young, and a number of record companies. Just starting out, Taki wasn't thoroughly satisfied with the nature of the work he was doing and explains that he was ''basically doing survival things. The confidence in myself wasn't really high.'' He was earning a living but finding it difficult to cope with the frantic pace and clutter that came with the work. Determined to regain his concentration and develop his style, he returned to Japan in 1977. His seven months there are in retrospect a watershed. ''That time was very good for me in a spiritual sense.'' It was also at this time that he met Lisa Powers.

Before meeting Taki Ono, Lisa was pursuing a career in fashion photography, a field in which she is still interested. "My first exposure to photography came in 1974. I was dating a photographer and he invited me into the darkroom." Whatever his intentions might have been, the result of that visit was an acute sense of aesthetic excitement: "I saw this image coming up in the tray, and I knew I wanted to do that." From there, she borrowed a camera, taught herself to use it and developed a philosophy. "I see my photographs in a film, as a frame of the film, and it's

very important for me to understand that there are moments that preceded this frame and there are moments that follow it, and this is just one frame that has a continuity."

Lisa had been given Taki's name by a friend. "We started seeing each other," she explains, "and then he came here and started working with me and then it just grew very organically. It was happening before we realized that it actually happened." The partnership has been extraordinarily successful. As photographer and artist, they complement each other in style and personality, and to-

gether create highly original and provocative work. "She has a great conceptual sense," Taki remarks. "Sometimes I get too abstract in my thinking and she brings me back down to earth. She clarifies what I'm doing."

Taki and Lisa have established no routine, preferring to allow their collaboration and each new idea the freedom to develop as it will. But the mystery stops here, for their work is widely regarded as the most exciting thing happening in illustration today, and each new product of their collaboration is eagerly awaited. "Whenever we see Roland on the street," Taki says, "he yells out, 'What are you doing here? Get back to work.'"

On the edge of a new decade, Taki Ono embodies the history and the future of airbrush art. A young man whose initial interest was draftsmanship, he has found—as did the Bauhaus masters—that a cooperative, creative effort enhances, rather than restricts, one's individual vision. And in applying the airbrush to photography, he has refashioned the concept of retouching into a remarkably innovative art form.

___ and... ___

Ten of the most successful illustrators in America—a tough act to follow. With artistic vision and technical expertise, they've given us wit and romance, futurism and nostalgia; they've undermined tradition and glorified sentiment. Influenced by various generations and nationalities, their art would seem to be the collective representation of all that is possible with an airbrush. Yet the following images bear witness to the contrary.

On newsstands and in record stores, on greeting cards and posters, the general public daily views, and is informed by, commercial art. As we have seen, the seventies was a decade of great popularity for the airbrush, and it would therefore be impossible, within the confines of one volume, to highlight *all* of the major exponents of this form. The illustrations on these pages, done by highly respected commercial artists, demonstrates the versatility and range of both the airbrush and the artists who have chosen to work with it.

Dave Wilcox   1974

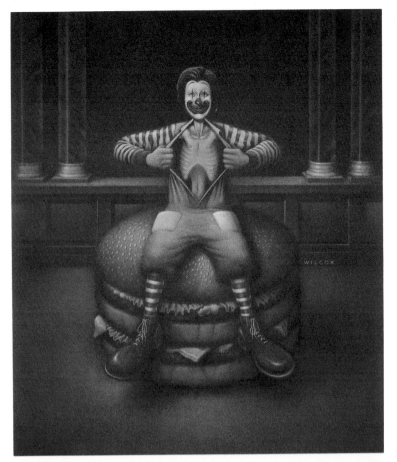

Dave Wilcox   1976

John Lykes   1979

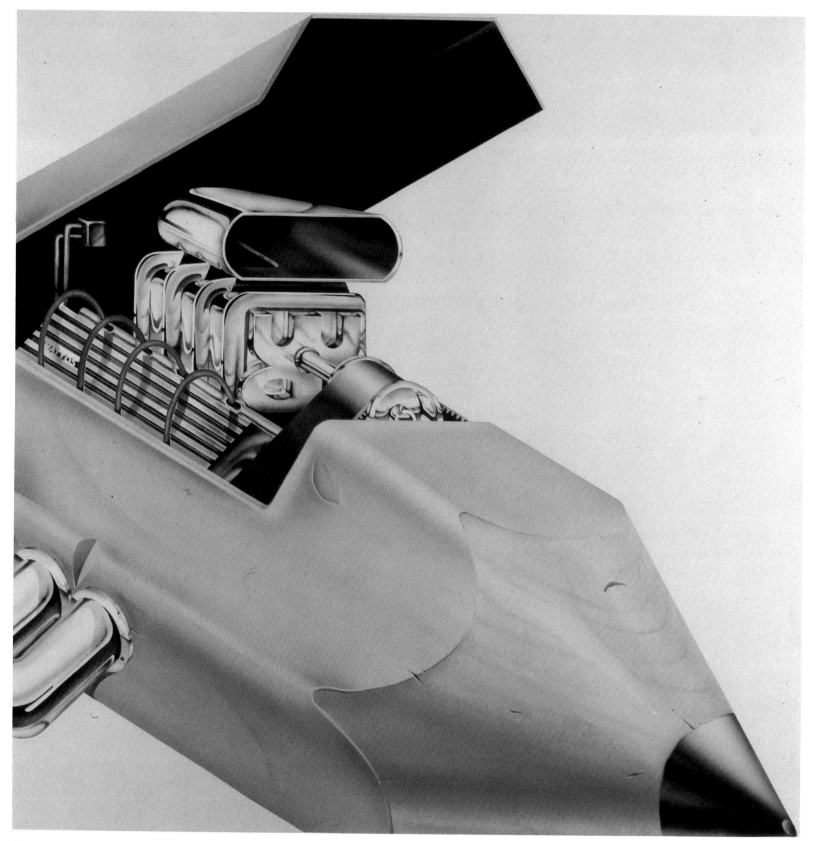

John Mattos   1978

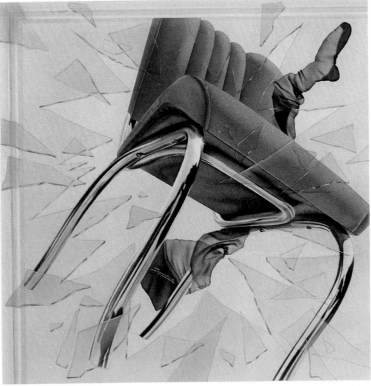

Ed Scarisbrick

Ed Scarisbrick   1978

179

Tom Nikosey   1978

Mac James   1978

Dave McMacken   1978

Dave McMacken   1978

Pamela Clare   1978

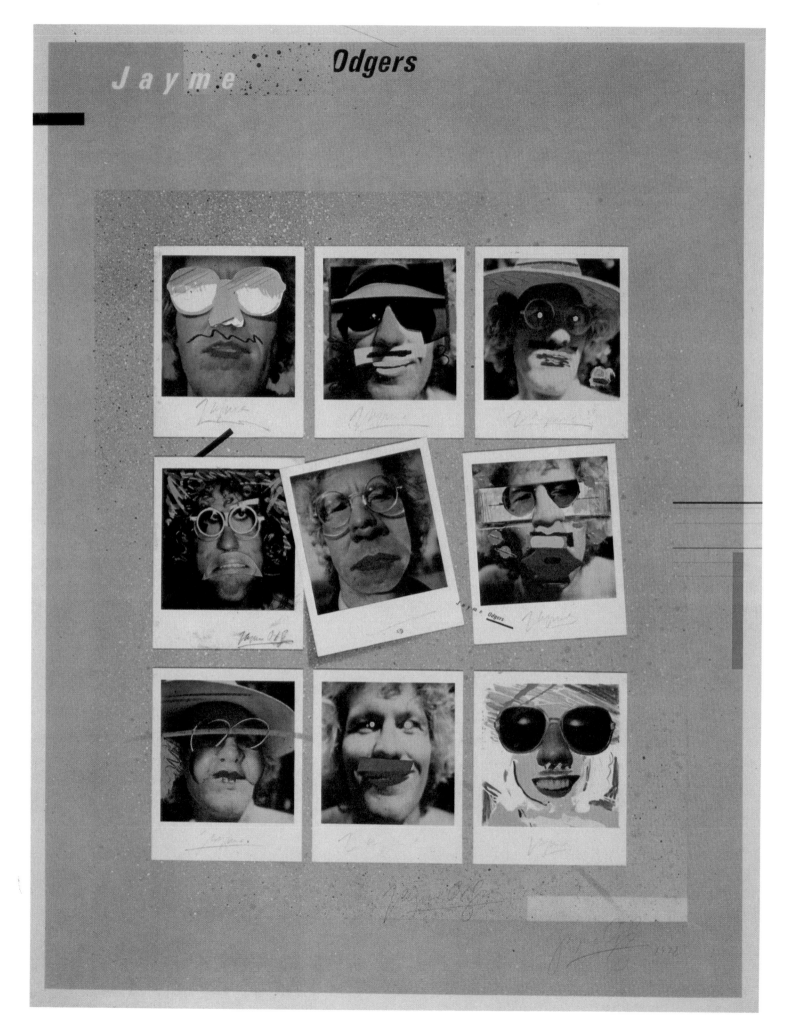

Louise Scott

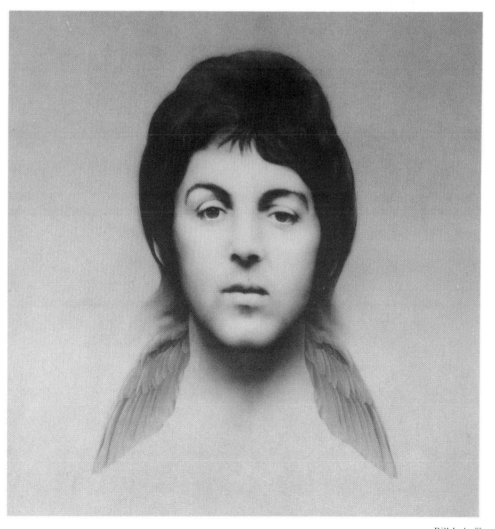

Bill Imhoff

185

Pater Sato   1977

Judy Markham   1978

189

Science Fiction: Fact and Fantasy

No brush strokes, no trails—just a clean, sharp picture that makes even imaginary worlds look real. It is no wonder that the airbrush is a primary tool in science-fiction art. Whether an illustration is intended to envision the future or interpret factual data, a sense of possibility is best achieved if the image reveals no one's hand—as if, indeed, the scene were photographed.

According to Lester Del Rey, an expert in the field, the first science-fiction piece was published by Hugo Gernsback, who "is generally recognized as the founder and foremost promoter." In the early twenties, Gernsback printed these stories in his technical magazines *Modern Electronics, Electrical Experimenter* and *Science and Invention.* His readers, avid enthusiasts of gadgetry and machines, responded eagerly to the new fiction, suggesting that a genre often associated with dreamers had in fact enjoyed its earliest popularity with those intrigued by facts and technology.

H. R. Giger

H. R. Giger

The airbrush also gained acceptance from people eager to embrace the use of machinery and has been put to great advantage in technical illustrations from *Fortune* covers to the modern day. *Amazing Stories,* the magazine that Gernsback started in 1926, was devoted to what was then called "scientifiction," and glorified the machine on its covers. "Whereas other fiction magazines of the time showed noble heroes and beauteous damsels (usually in distress)," wrote Lester Del Rey, "*Amazing Stories* and the magazines that followed depicted the wonderful world of the machine." The best of science-fiction art, then, has its roots in technical illustration. And though the early sci-fi stories are now considered singularly flat, much of the art retains its appeal.

The fact that science fiction doesn't simply come out of the blue is illustrated by the work of Don Dixon. Work-

ing cooperatively with the most knowledgeable scientists of the space age, Dixon renders his awesome images of projected reality with the airbrush. A typical description of one of his "Spacescapes": "Halley's Comet—Possible scene from an orbital station in 1986, when the famous comet is due to return to the warmer regions of the solar system." Indeed, this "possible scene" is hard to distinguish from a photograph.

Science fiction carries an accent over both words. It juxtaposes the imagined with the known, and successful science-fiction illustration communicates that mixture. Man as machine, man in middle earth, man on the moon— vague possibilities and historical truths that recall the motto of *Amazing Stories:* "Extravagant fiction today . . . Cold fact tomorrow!"

Sushei Nagaoka   1978

Sushei Nagaoka   1978

Jupiter Seen from Europa   Second of Jupiter's large satellites, Europa completes its orbit in about 3.6 days. Its diameter is 3,050 kilometers and its density is 3.3 times that of water, so it seems to be similar in nature to our own moon. Unlike the moon, however, Europa seems to have a thin crust of water ice and a tenuous atmosphere. Seen from Europa's equator, Jupiter (12° in apparent diameter) rides majestically in a faintly glowing sky as an inner satellite, Io, transits.

Formation of Crater Tycho   One of the most spectacular lunar features is Tycho, which dominates the southern hemisphere of the full moon with its dazzling impact basin and ejecta rays. Formed perhaps as "recently" as 50 million years ago, Tycho is the result of a disagreement over right-of-way between our satellite and a planetisimal perhaps 5 kilometers across. Impacting with a speed of tens-of-kilometers per second, the kinetic energy of the planetoid may have been equal to 1,000 hydrogen bombs.

Cygnus X-1   Possibly the aftermath of a supernova. In the picture, the large blue star is attended by the remnant of a star that exploded so violently that its core was crushed to the point at which gravitational collapse began; it could no longer support its own weight. Gravity at the surface of the collapsing core eventually grew so strong that nothing—not even light—could escape from it, and it became a "black hole." Now it sweeps about its erstwhile companion like a cosmic vacuum cleaner, draining away the star's matter.

Orion Nebula   Each of the myriad stars that we see in the night sky is a sun, and many are far larger and more brilliant than the particularly close star we call the Sun. All stars probably have their origin in immense clouds of dust and gas similar to the Orion Nebula, here seen from the vicinity of an earthlike planet in the outer fringes of the nebulosity. From such a vantage point, an observer might watch the process of star formation as, over a period of perhaps only a few thousand years, dark globules of matter within the nebula slowly contract under the pull of their own gravitation, becoming hotter as they grow more compact, until eventually nuclear processes are triggered in their cores and they light up.

Capture of the Moon   Prior to 3 billion years ago, the Moon may have been a planet in its own right, following an independent orbit about the sun. If this theory is true, the Moon may have been captured by Earth's gravity when it passed near Earth and was slowed by friction with a ring of debris still orbiting the planet.

Birth of the Sun   To conserve angular momentum, the cloud spun as it collapsed—at first slowly, then with increasing speed (just as a pirouetting figure skater spins more quickly when she pulls in her arms). After perhaps a few million years, the cloud flattened into a disk. At the center, where the hydrogen was most concentrated and collisions between particles most frequent, the temperature soared, until at some point nuclear fusion processes began and the Sun lit up. In a slow-motion expansion, the solar wind drove the un-assimilated gas and dust further into space, exposing the orbiting belt of matter that would someday become the planet Earth.

Mars Vertical View   Viewed from 1,600 km (1,000 mi), Martian topography becomes apparent: craters, some fresh and sharp, some filled in with drifting sand . . . volcanoes, miles high, with "lee waves" of ice crystals streaming from the summits, caused by warm air rising up the flanks and being abruptly chilled . . . and, most intriguing, dry riverbeds, cut by running water in a time when Mars had a more temperate climate.

Titan   Saturn's largest moon—5,600 km in diameter—seems to have a fairly substantial atmosphere of methane and hydrogen (possibly replenished by "spinoff" from Saturn itself) and may be covered with reddish-brown clouds of such substances as ammonium hydrosulfide. Dr. Carl Sagan has suggested that because of the "greenhouse effect," Titan may be warm enough to support some form of life.

—Dixon

195

Charlie Wild and Bob Zoell 1979

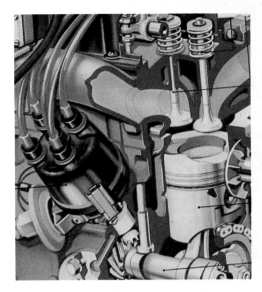

Technical

A technical illustration is a three-dimensional representation of a machine, or an industrial or biological process. Generally used for instructional purposes, advertising or product display, technical illustrations sometimes serve as models for machines that have not yet been constructed. The airbrush, by itself or in conjunction with a photograph, is often the tool used to render this exacting illustration.

As a cross section of a product that will be viewed by students, prospective buyers or manufacturers, it is imperative that the technical illustration be clear and understandable. Not only must it convey the function, but it must do so in a way that is immediately accessible and pleasing to look at—comprising, after all, a visual explanation of how something works. Perhaps the most demanding of airbrush work, the successful technical illustration is made up of fine shading, definite contrasts and precise linear rules. Working from a blueprint, photograph or the object itself, the illustrator must put minute detail to aesthetic effect, making the engine of a motorcycle, for instance, appear clean, sensible, and depending on the eye of the beholder, even attractive.

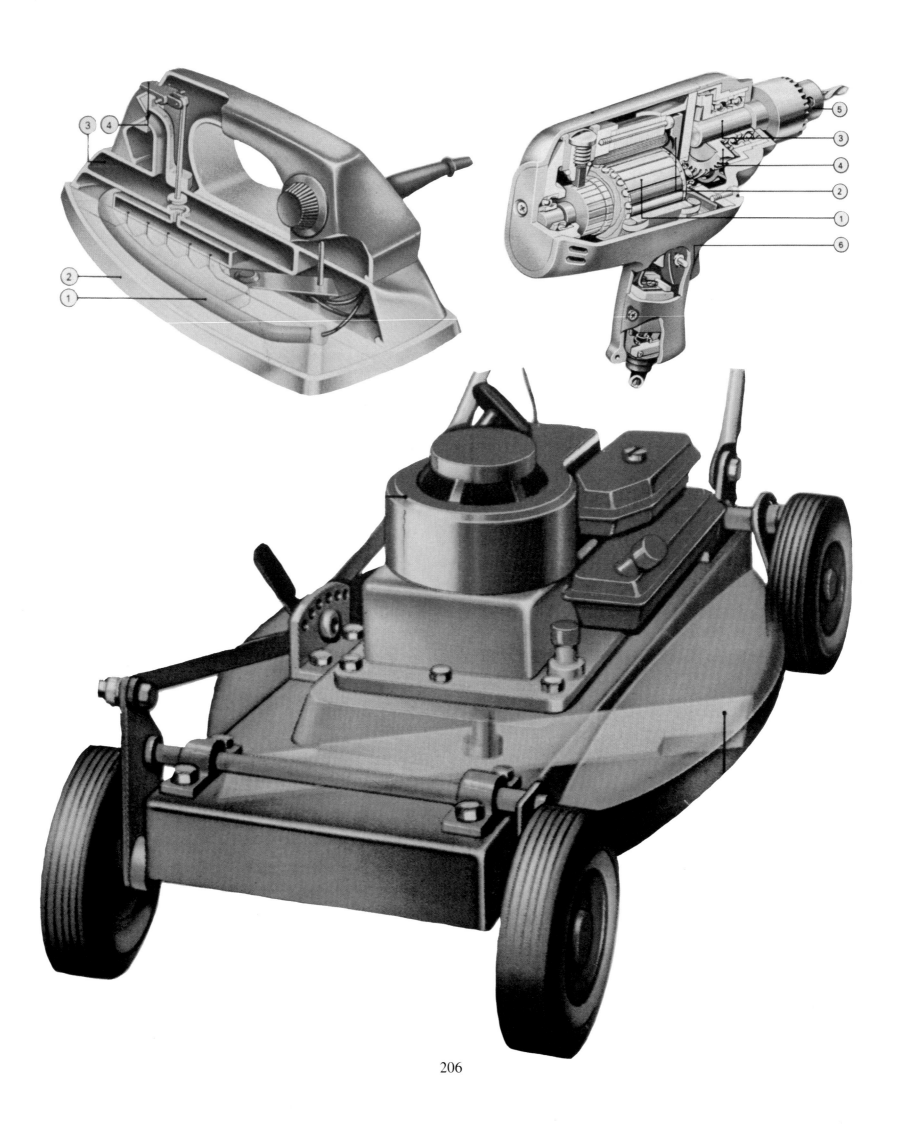

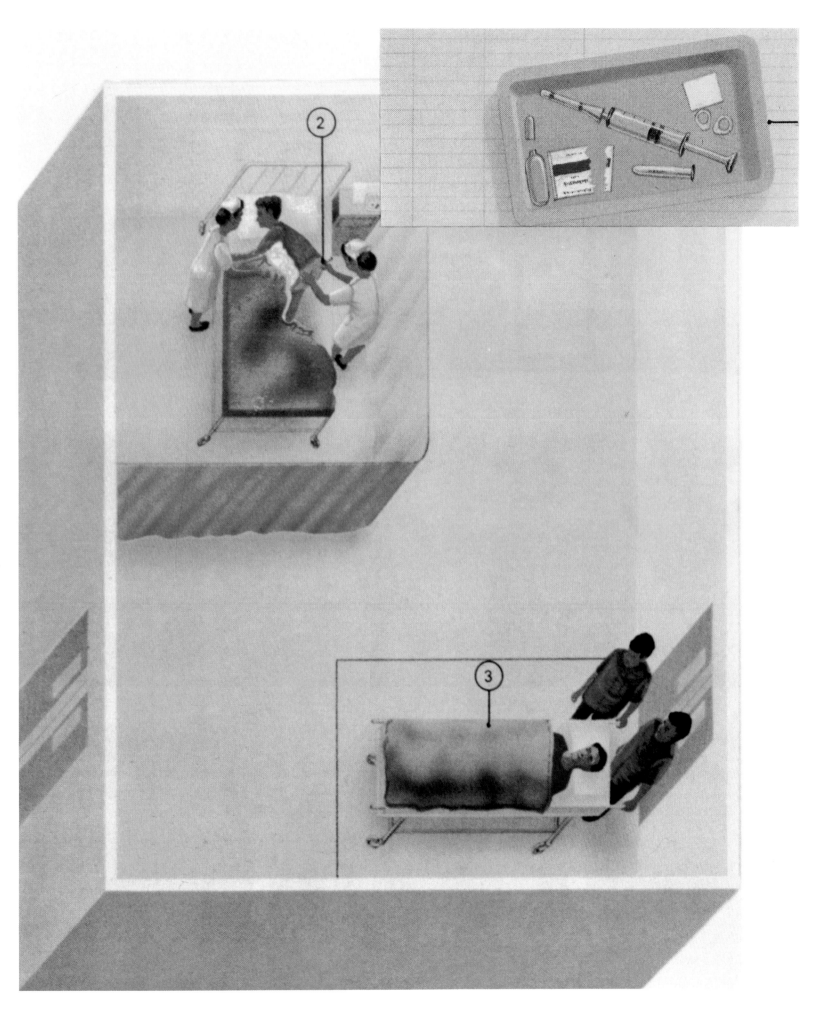

Behind the Scenes

In tracing the development of popular illustration, it would be negligent to omit the all-important role of the art director. Beginning with the emergence of lavish consumer magazines in the late twenties and sustained today in the advertising and music industries, the influence of the men and women behind the scenes has been everywhere visible, though often overlooked.

The chief responsibility of the job is the selection and coordination of imagery, but the extent to which any given art director's vision becomes integrated into public taste depends, of course, on the individual talent at hand. Because popular acceptance of airbrush art has, historically, varied wildly, the medium is particularly indebted to the art directors who have given it their endorsement.

MAGAZINES   With the first issue of Henry Luce's *Fortune* in February 1930, a new means of communication was established between buyer and seller. Though not strictly a consumer magazine, *Fortune* bridged the gap between these mutually dependent economic groups by informing the public—through studiously researched and handsomely printed articles—of how Big Business operated. Despite the impending Depression, no cost was spared in fulfilling Luce's desire for beautifully incorporated artwork. Among the illustrations of industrial scenes that graced the pages and covers of *Fortune* were those of airbrush artists Joseph Binder and George Giusti.

Subscribing to a similarly extravagant approach to publishing, Condé Nast directed his *Vogue, Vanity Fair* and *House and Garden* at the elite few who could afford the luxury goods that were elegantly displayed in those publications. Nast, who had a strong background in advertising, did more than anyone else to develop the concept of the consumer magazine. "One must set Condé Nast apart from the other merchant publishers," wrote Theodore Peterson in *Magazines in the Twentieth Century.* "Through his magazines, he coached Americans in high fashion and gracious living for more than thirty years." For his art director, Nast chose Mehemed Fehmy Agha, a Russian-Turk whose influence led, declared the *Fifty-first Annual of Ads* in 1971, "to a fundamental change in modern publication design and the consequent transformation of the role, importance and contribution of the art director in editorial planning and organization."

Dr. Agha, as he came to be called, assumed the art directorship of *Vogue* in 1929. He brought to the job a strong background in science, photography, typography and fine arts, and thereby introduced to American publishing the active participation of the art director at every level. No longer would pictures be added as mere decoration after the fact; as initiated by Agha, magazine illustrations would be an organic part of editorial planning. His insistence on pictorial excellence was perhaps best reflected in the pages of *Vanity Fair,* a Condé Nast publication dedicated to cultural pursuits, where Agha was also art director. Because of the prevalence of simple lines and graceful contours in the thirties, and because Dr. Agha worked tirelessly to achieve a beautifully printed page, airbrush artists were pleased to fill the demand for their paintings in these magazines; thus the sleek airbrush look became associated with the tasteful elegance of the period.

A major competitor of the Nast empire was William Randolph Hearst's *Harper's Bazaar.* A fashion magazine, *Harper's* was distinguished by its fine fiction until 1934, when Alexey Brodovitch came from Paris to take on the duties of art director. He remained with the magazine until 1959, and a recent article remarked that his tenure was "a veritable Periclean age for the publication. The magazine's effect on editorial design, style, conception, taste and visual intellect continues to resonate throughout the broad compass of editorial design."

Brodovitch saw publicity as far more than a simple matter of selling a product, regarding it instead as "full of contrast and paradox. Publicity is born of life and life is learned through publicity.... If we think of Publicity as art...we should call it Deep Art as in contrast to the term Fine Art." Nearly obsessed with the notion of change, Brodovitch sought to convey in each issue of *Harper's* a sense of the dramatic advances made in the modern world; his intellectual energy transferred onto his work this acute sensitivity to everything around him. One of the exciting new forms of illustration that he advocated was airbrush art.

Bob Cato, a successful art director in Los Angeles, worked over the years with Brodovitch, who remained in New York. And much as the latter was inspired by Sergei Diaghilev of the Ballet Russe, so was Cato greatly influenced by Brodovitch. "He had the ability to reflect what he had experienced in the Russian Ballet; his pages became theater pieces. There is a concern for space and time and color and movement throughout his magazines. He was the first art director who laid a magazine on the floor and moved the pages about to get the flow and essence of an extraordinary look. He knew what pages ought to have a tremendous amount of energy, and what pages ought to be very placid, very beautiful, or very moving. . . . It was what he called 'graphic journalism,' not art directing.'' Cato's reverence supports the recorded observation that ''Brodovitch was perhaps the single most powerful influence on the development of practicing artists, designers, and photographers of his time, and he left us an incomparable legacy of living talent.'' In the hands of Alexey Brodovitch, *Harper's Bazaar* became a beautifully illustrated magazine whose advertising was at least as striking as its editorial content.

By 1933 it was clear that there was a market for women's fashion magazines. Then David Smart, a shrewd young advertising executive, decided to expand that market with the creation of *Esquire,* one of the most successful publications of the decade. In addition to the high standards of its literary material and the groundbreaking promotion of men's fashions, *Esquire* became famous for its full-page color—and off-color—cartoons. ''Probably no other American magazine had ever been so laden with artwork,'' wrote Theodore Peterson. *Esquire* also introduced to American culture the airbrushed Petty Girl of George Petty. With the initiation of the double fold-out in the December 1939 issue, the Petty Girl became a full-fledged piece of Americana, and the artist much sought after. Just when the powers behind the magazine became increasingly frustrated by Petty's rapidly inflating ego, an alternative appeared in the form of Alberto Vargas, who needed a job. In the end, the Varga (later Vargas) Girl was more than a replacement. Smart, the publisher and owner, and Arnold Gingrich, the editor, made all the editorial decisions at *Esquire.* And though Smart's business methods were later brought into question, it was his ingenuity and business savvy that propelled the pinup girl into the public consciousness.

Aside from *Esquire,* most men's magazines were predominantly concerned with outdoor sports—hunting, fishing and mountain climbing. In *Playboy,* Hugh Hefner wanted to emphasize indoor sports. In the early fifties, only a few years out of the University of Illinois, Hefner wrote to a friend: ''I'd like to produce an entertainment magazine for the city-bred guy—breezy and sophisticated. The girlie features would guarantee the initial sale but the magazine would have quality too.'' One of the reasons the girlie feature itself attained quality was the eventual participation of Alberto Vargas.

Having suffered a traumatic parting of the ways with David Smart, Vargas was by the early fifties once again in need of work. And in 1959 Reid Austin became the associate art director for *Playboy.* ''I've always been passionate for Vargas,'' Austin said in a 1975 interview. ''As a Boy Scout, I became familiar with his work [while] collecting magazines in wartime scrap drives. My life was never the same.'' It is largely due to Austin's influence that Vargas became a regular contributor to *Playboy* and that the airbrushed Vargas Girl continues to be a favorite image of feminine beauty.

With the conception of *Life* and *Look* magazines in 1936, photo journalism was born. Just as publisher Henry Luce had pioneered lavish illustration with *Fortune,* he now inaugurated the use of what he called ''the mind-guided camera.'' Stories would be told in words *and* pictures, fastidiously arranged for the greatest impact on the reader, and produced by a team of picture editor, photographer, researcher and writer. ''The picture magazine was the result of at least five influences,'' Theodore Peterson concluded. ''The illustrated weeklies at home, the illustrated magazines from abroad, the movies, the tabloid newspapers and advertising photography all combined to produce the picture magazine. They were helped by technological advances in printing and photography.''

The airbrush, ever-present as a retouching tool, was relegated to this use during the reign of the photograph. It was not until the mid-sixties that its artistic capabilities were once again embraced—and this, thanks primarily to the insight of an art director.

When Mike Salisbury took over as art director of *West* magazine in 1967, the management—the Los Angeles *Times*—had strict policies about the ratio of photographs to illustrations. Coming from a job in advertising, Salisbury found the year-old magazine ''totally lackluster'' and wanting in excitement. With single-minded dedication, he set out to make *West* a magazine of, for and about Los Angeles. ''I started becoming almost like a historian of L.A. The strongest period for the city was the thirties and forties; it was in its real glory then and airbrush art represented the feeling of that time.'' For Salisbury, the modern designs of airbrush artists like Robert Grossman, Dave

Willardson and Bob Zoell combined with the streamlined Deco look of early airbrushing to form the imagery of Los Angeles.

While older art directors dismissed the airbrush as wartime nostalgia, Salisbury recognized its potential for innovative graphic ideas. He was the first to publish this new look and, as Willardson has said, "Appearing in *West* was like an endorsement." As other art directors, like Jean Paul Goude at *Esquire* and Roland Young at Capitol Records, enlisted the work of these illustrators, airbrush art left the realm of nostalgia and became an integral part of culture in the seventies.

THE MUSIC INDUSTRY   In 1967 a new phenomenon appeared in the music industry: the record-album package. Though some classical and a few jazz albums had previously enjoyed more than the customary functional wrapping, the revolution inspired by the Beatles and psychedelia in general expanded to include the art that advertised the music. Musicians now were courted, rather than tolerated, by record companies and could demand contracts, rehearsal time and artistic control of their products. Albums, from first groove to graphics, were no longer a random collection of songs, but a carefully designed totality.

Buying albums became a recreational activity, something to do on a Saturday afternoon. Coming home, you'd settle down, turn the volume up, listen to the music and study the album jacket. An astonishing number of those jackets were, and continue to be, airbrush art. Fanciful or familiar, sentimental or sensational, this enormously versatile instrument was the medium chosen by the art directors for the rock-'n-roll message.

Bob Cato was in on the early stages of the album package. Indeed, at Columbia Records in 1959 he proposed the unprecedented concept of letting the recording artist in on the artwork. Columbia was at first reluctant but they gave it a shot, and Cato was the man in charge; for his first assignment, he was sent from New York to California. "I was told that they had just signed an extraordinary artist and that we would have to break him to the world. His name was Igor Stravinsky." While working with the maestro, Cato received a call to rush back to New York to promote yet another discovery—Miles Davis. By meeting and talking to the musicians themselves, Cato initiated the practice of serving the musical art with the graphic art. As

we have seen, it was several years before the idea became universal.

Cato's earliest recollection of airbrushing goes back to the *Esquire* days when his wife, then a model, was one of the first Varga girls. He subsequently used the tool while working with Brodovitch on fashion illustration at *Harper's*. Though primarily a magazine man, Cato is also intrigued with bringing music and art together in album design. And "Of all the graphics produced in the world, albums have the longest shelf life; they have the longest life span of any commercial art form that's ever been created."

Roland Young, who filled in at *West* whenever Salisbury was on vacation, was responsible for carrying the new look in graphics from publishing to record-packaging; his enthusiasm for airbrush work contributed immensely to its eventual proliferation in records. "We had a lot of ideas about graphics in the sixties. When the lyrics and the music began to say things, our ideas finally came through. If there hadn't been a *West* magazine, those ideas would still be sitting there."

Ed Thrasher was among the first art directors to apply the airbrush look to the new music, in keeping with his conviction that "the criteria for a good art director is always to be there first." In 1969, he was there. Working for Warner Bros., he approached the album jacket as something that would motivate a person to notice one particular record among the others. And the airbrush "had a lightness to it that was refreshing. It went with the music that was changing at that time too."

Hailing from South Africa, Rod Dyer was drawn to airbrushing because it had a "pop feel that was kind of fun." With a constant workload of three or four album covers per week, Rod Dyer Inc. employs fourteen designers and production people and is involved in the entire merchandising of an album—cover, billboards and posters. And the studio has to work fast. "What usually happens," he explains, "is that the record company will call us in, and we'll listen to some of the music. The group will give us some direction, and then we'll suggest concepts. If they like our layouts, we proceed. From concept to photography normally takes about two weeks." This remarkable pace apparently works well, for both the art and the artist. As Mick Haggerty, a former member of Dyer's staff, says, "He really does a lot for people, and has helped a hell of a lot of artists. He doesn't suck them up and use them up either. It's very much an open situation."

Yet another European import, German-born Ria Lewerke started her own company after five years at United Artists. It was at U.A. that she came under the tutelage of Mike Salisbury and, through him, became aware of airbrush art. "He was using Willardson a lot. I love music, and the art related so well to rock-'n-roll. It's very dynamic, and just sparkles somehow." Thus she was hooked by the airbrush and by the career of art direction. "I'm an idea person. I like to work with people and I like to direct." Being both foreigner and female, Lewerke had to fight just a little bit harder to become a well-paid art director; as evidenced by the design firm bearing her name, the fight was worth it. Undoubtedly there are still a few male artists who resist taking direction from a woman. Of them she light-heartedly observes, "The ones that don't like it just go away."

THE ART'S DIRECTION   According to those who brought about the sixties' revival, airbrush art will not go away. But its imagery will change dramatically. "One thing that could happen is that the airbrush will take over photography," suggests Roland Young, currently an art di-rector at A & M Records. "It will require an incredible amount of draftsmanship and artistry."

Young envisions the return of the sketch artist: using live models, setting up scenes, first drawing and then color-ing with the airbrush. The artistry is in capturing the per-sonality of the subject. "I see little germs of it happening already. You can see airbrushed cars in magazine ads. An airbrushed car is much more romantic than a photographed car." It isn't nostalgia that he's after; the overall style might be romantic, but the situations set up by the artist would communicate real life—not unlike the "outmoded" cam-era. With the future of graphics so firmly pictured in his mind, why does Young feel that this new look won't emerge until the mid-eighties? "It's well defined, but I have to wait for the music to catch up. Things have to synchronize. When it happens, we'll be ready."

Even the most innovative art director is quick to con-cede that predicting the future is chancy at best, and Young is no exception. From Mick Haggerty's visible strokes to Taki Ono's blending of photograph and airbrush, experi-mentation is nothing if not diverse. Ed Thrasher offers an understated summation of what we can expect: "There are always so many things that can be done, so it's just a matter of revolution, isn't it?"

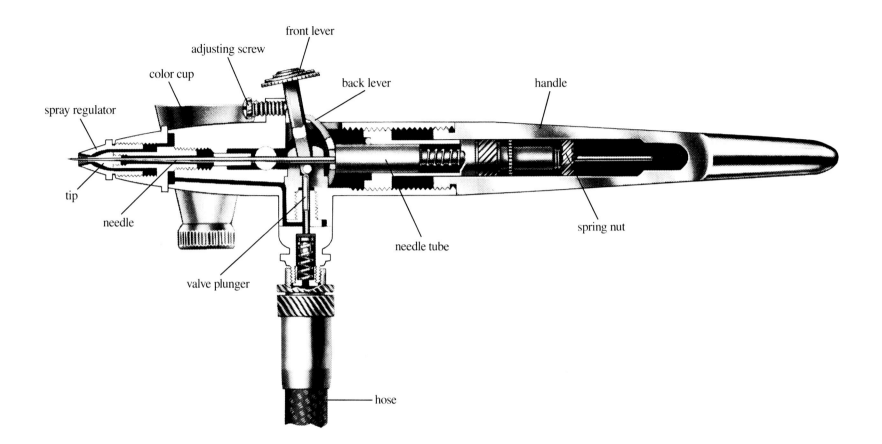

For the person interested in learning how to operate an airbrush, there are several in-depth brochures and manuals currently on the market. Obviously, we cannot give a detailed account of the methodology in this volume. On the following pages, however, the reader can follow the step-by-step procedure of rendering an airbrush illustration.

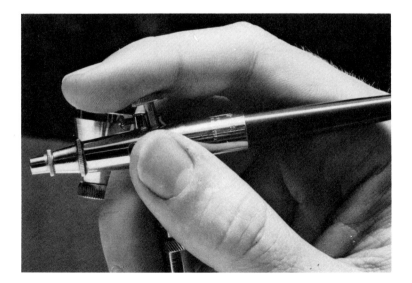

Pushing down on the trigger releases only air, not paint.

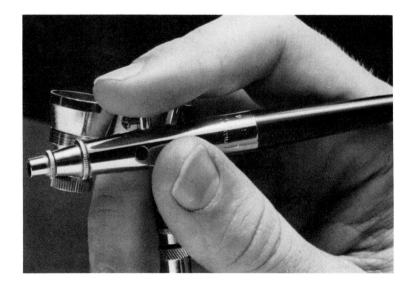

With the trigger still held down, pulling back slowly and evenly on the trigger releases the paint gradually.

After the requisite meetings with the art director, a concept has been developed, and research completed. The artist begins to sketch out the material for the illustration.

Finishing touches are applied to the sketch on tracing paper. The drawing is then outlined and transferred to illustration board.

A transparent adhesive film called *frisket paper* is placed over the entire drawing. This will protect those areas that are not being airbrushed at any given time. The swivel knife (a rotating blade that moves easily with the turn of the wrist) cuts into the frisket paper, baring that portion of the drawing that is to be airbrushed.

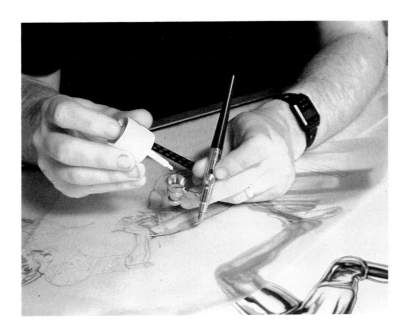

The pigment is applied to the color cup. Dyes are often used in airbrushing because of their color brilliance, water solubility and transparent layering effects. The artist will push down on the lever for air and pull back on the lever for paint. Most airbrushes operate on this double-action principle, allowing for a desirable mixture of pigment and air.

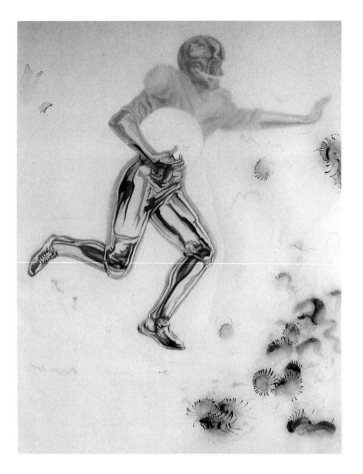

The swivel knife cuts into the frisket paper, revealing only the section that was to be airbrushed.

The illustration is meticulously built up, area by area.

The illustration as it appears before the final touches.

The frisket paper is peeled off to reveal a clean crisp illustration. Note the contrast of the splattered area which has been protected by the frisket.

THE
LINDSAY TROPHY

Thus the elements combine to result in a completed airbrush illustration. We wish to thank airbrush artist Ed Scarisbrick for his cooperation in putting together this brief pictorial presentation.

Picture Credits

Page Number
Date
Title of Piece
Artist
Art Director
Client

8
1979
TV Head
Taki Ono: Photo, Lisa Powers
Wet Magazine

10
1979
Red Lips
Ed Scarisbrick

14
1979
Caveman
Rick Probst
W. Scott Griffiths
Richard H. Childers Productions

78
1967
Johnson
Robert Grossman
Dougald Stermer
Ramparts

79
1976
nose
Robert Grossman

79
1970
Girl
Robert Grossman
Milton Glaser
Audience Magazine

80
1968
Sunshine Lake
Skip Andrews
Lanning Stern, Skip Andrews

80
1969
Suds
Lanning Stern
Mike Salisbury
West Magazine

81
1969
Football
Lanning Stern

82
1969
Earthquake
Lanning Stern
Skip Andrews, Lanning Stern

83
1970
Donkey
Ed Mel
Skip Andrews

83
1970
Porkey
Ed Mel
Skip Andrews
Life Magazine

84
1975
Nude
Ed Mel

85
1970
Over Head
Frank Mel

86
1977
Modern Chair (Detail)
John Van Hamersveld
John Van Hamersveld
Loyalla Museum Of Contemporary Art

86
1976
Airflo Poster
John Van Hamersveld
John Van Hamersveld
Fortress INC

86
1973
Southern Calif
John Van Hamersveld
Ed Thrasher
Warner Brothers

87
1976
Bad Poster
John Van Hamersveld
John Van Hamersveld
New World Picture

91
1979
Screaming Face
Gary Panter
Gary Panter
Richard H. Childers Productions

102
1970
Vietnam Moratorium Poster (Detail)
Bob Zoell
Lanning Stern
Vietnam Moratorium

104
1970
All Kinds Comix
Bob Zoell
Al Deveron, Bob Zoell
Promethian Enterprises

105
1970
Have A Heart
Bob Zoell
Lanning Stern, Ed Meter
Vietnam Moratorium

106
1975
Bird Close Pins
Bob Zoell
Bob Zoell

106
1975
Crows
Bob Zoell
Bob Zoell

107
1975
Dancing Rainbows
Bob Zoell
Bob Zoell

107
1979
Business Cards
Bob Zoell
Bob Zoell

108
1969, 1979
Kitchen Safety
Bob Zoell

109
1977, 1979
Self Portrait
Bob Zoell
Bob Zoell

110
1975
Humpty Dumpty (Detail)
Charles White
Pete Catroulis

112
1975
Ladies and Gentlemen:
    The Rolling Stones
Charles White III
Roland Binzen
Rolling Stones

112
1974
Octopus
Charles White III
John Berg
Colombia Records

113
1975
Humpty Dumpty
Charles White III
Pete Catroulis

113
1974
Running Crome Man
Charles White III
Charles White III
Ancorp Co. logo

114
1975
Metal Door
Charles White III
Charles White III
Charles White III

115
1977
Chrome Bumper
Charles White III
Eiko Tshioka
Yaseijidai

218

Page Number
Date
Title of Piece
Artist
Art Director
Client

178
1978
Competition
John Mattos
Mark Anderson
Western Art Directors Club

179
Sept. 1978
Chair
Ed Scarisbrick
Mike Doud
AGI

179
Jan. 1978
——
Ed Scarisbrick
Bill Skirsky
Chic

180
Jan. 1978
Let it flow
Todd Schorr
Carin Goldberg
CBS Records

180
1973
Base Ball
Ed Kasper
Richard Gangel
Sports Illustrated

181
Nov. 1976
Sargent Peppers
Tom Nikosey
Susan Herr
RSO Records

181
1978
A & M Records Corporate Identity
Mac James
Roland Young
A & M Records

182
1978
1941
Dave McMacken
Dan Perry and Dave McMacken
Steven Spielberg

182
1978
Lady Lynda
Dave McMacken
Dave McMacken and Tony Laine
CBS Records

183
1978
Sahara Vision
Pamela Clare
Pamela Clare
Self

184
1978
Self Portrait Series
Jayme Odgers
Jayme Odgers
Jayme Odgers

185
1978
Hiro Sushi
Louise Scott
Hiro Sushi Restaurant

185
1977
Paul McCartney
Bill Imhoff
Virginia Team
Rolling Stone

186
1977
Pater's Space
Pater Sato
Pater Sato
Polydor (Japan)

187
Nov. 1978
Girl In Chair
Judy Markham
Cathy Philpott
Chic Magazine

188
1979
Robot
Jim Evans
Richard Childers
Richard H. Childers Productions

189
1979
Robot
Jim Evans
Richard Childers
Richard H. Childers Productions

190
—
—
Adrian Chesterman

191
—
—
Angus McKie

192
—
—
H. R. Giger

193
1977
ELO
Shusei Nagaoka
Ria Lewerke
Jet Records

193
1978
Technical Spaceship
Shusei Nagaoka
Henry Viccara
Casablanca Records

194
1977
Jupiter Seen from Europa
Don Dixon
Don Dixon
Dixon Spacescapes

194
1977
Formation of Crater Tycho
Don Dixon
Don Dixon
Dixon Spacescapes

194
1975
Cygnus X-1
Don Dixon
Don Dixon
Dixon Spacescapes

194
1974
Orion Nebula
Don Dixon
Don Dixon
Dixon Spacescapes

195
1975
Capture of the Moon
Don Dixon
Don Dixon
Dixon Spacescapes

195
1975
Birth of the Sun
Don Dixon
Don Dixon
Dixon Spacescapes

195
1974
Mars Vertical View
Don Dixon
Don Dixon
Dixon Spacescapes

195
1974
Titan
Don Dixon
Don Dixon
Dixon Spacescapes

199
1979
Einstein Retouched
Bob Zoell, Charlie Wild
Bob Zoell
Richard H. Childers Productions

200
1978
Superman
Rob Friedman
Warner Brothers
Thought Factory

204
1978
Red Bike
Shusei Nagaoka

Honda

205
1976
Blue Bike
Shusei Nagaoka
Paul R. Halesworth
Suzuki/Cycle Magazine

In most instances, unattributed illustrations are within the public domain, and information about them unavailable. Any omission of credit is inadvertent and will be corrected in future printings if notification is sent to the publisher.

Allner, W. H., "Jean Carlu," *Graphis* (1947).
———, *Posters.* New York, 1952.
Battersby, Martin, *The Decorative Twenties.* New York, 1969.
Bayer, Herbert; Gropius, Walter; and Gropius, Ise, *Bauhaus.* New York, 1938.
Bayer, Herbert, *Herbert Bayer.* New York, 1967.
Binder, Carla, *Joseph Binder.* Vienna, 1976.
Brodovitch, Alexey, "What Pleases the Modern Man." *Commercial Art,* (1933).
Brunhammer, Yvonne, *The Nineteen Twenties Style.* London, 1969.
Corthine, Stanley, "The Airbrush and Its Uses." *Commercial Art Magazine,* (1933).
Del Rey, Lester, ed., *Fantastic Science-Fiction-Art 1926–1954,* New York, 1975.
Drake, Chas F., "Gunning For Gum Sales." *Art and Industry* (1937). *The Encyclopedia of Photography,* Willard D. Morgan, ed. New York, 1968.
Ferebee, Ann, *A History of Design from the Victorian Era to the Present.* New York, 1970.
Fern, Alan M., *Word and Image.* New York, 1968.
Frazer, Samuel W., and Stine, George F., *A Treatise on the Airbrush.* Boston, 1930.
Frenzel, H. K., "George Salter." *Gebrauchsgraphik* (1932).
"Garretto 35," *Gebrauchsgraphik* (June 1935).
Gaunt, W., "The Whole World of Advertising." *Commercial Art* (October 1929).
Greer, Carl, *Handbook of Advertising and Printing.* New York, 1931.
Hamill, Pete, "Robert Grossman." *Graphis* #186 ('76–'77).
Haworth-Booth, Mark, "E. McKnight Kauffer." *The Penrose Annual* #64, 1971.
Hillier, Bevis, *The Decorative Arts of the Forties and Fifties.* New York, 1975.
Hornung, Clarence P., and Johnson, Fridolf, *200 Years of American Graphics Art.* New York, 1976.
Hulett, Steve, "A Star Is Drawn." *Film Comment* (February, 1979).
Jelinek, J., *The Pictorial Encyclopedia of the Evolution of Man.* London, 1975.
Kauffer, E. McKnight, and Huxley, Aldous, "A Word About E. McKnight Kauffer." *PM* (March 1937).

Laming, Annette, *Lascaux: Paintings and Engravings.* London, 1959.
McMullan, James, "How Artists Learn About Reality." *Print* (January/February, 1978).
Marshack, Alexander, "Exploring the Mind of Ice Age Man." *National Geographic,* Vol. 147, No. 1 (January 1975).
Maurello, S. Ralph, *Commercial Art Techniques.* New York, 1952.
———, *The Complete Airbrush Book.* New York, 1955.
Metzl, Ervine, *The Poster: Its History and Its Art.* New York, 1963.
Morgan, Willard D., ed., *The Encyclopedia of Photography,* New York, 1968.
Naylor, Gillian, *The Bauhaus.* London, 1968.
Neumann, Eckhard, *Functional Graphic Design in the 20's.* New York, 1967.
New York Art Directors Club, "Alexey Brodovitch," and "Mehemed Fehmy Agha," *The 51st Annual of Ads,* 1971.
Oeri, Georgine, "George Giusti." *Graphis* #26, (1949).
Peterson, Theodore, *Magazines in the Twentieth Century,* Urbana, Illinois, 1964.
Powell, T. G. E., *Prehistoric Art.* New York, 1966.
Rhodes, Anthony, *Propaganda: The Art of Persuasion: World War II.* New York, 1976.
Ross, Shelley, "Alberto Vargas," *Biography News,* July/August, 1975.
Rossi, Attilio, *Posters.* London, 1966.
Rotzler, Willy, "Osterwalder." *Graphis* #148 ('70–'71).
Scheffauer, E. T., trans., "Jean Carlu." *Gebrauchsgraphik* (January 1935).
Sembach, Klaus-Jurgen, *Style 1930.* New York, 1971.
Shepard, Otis, "Posters in the United States of America." *Commercial Art* (December, 1933).
Stote, Amos, "Jean Carlu." *Print* (Spring 1942).
Tobias, J. Carroll, *A Manual of Airbrush Technique.* Boston, 1946.
Tritton, Ronald, "Abram Games." *Graphis* (1947).
Vargas, Alberto, and Austin, Reid, *Vargas,* New York, 1978.
Vergani, Orio, "Paolo Garretto." *Graphis* #20 (1947).
Walters, Thomas, *Art Deco.* London, 1973.

A Note from the Producer

I've always had a certain fascination with books. As a child, I used to hide under the covers with my Cub Scout flashlight, reading exciting tales of black horses on desert islands. When, in September of 1978, I perceived the need for a book on airbrush art, I jumped at the chance, and now, nine months later, this book is complete. It took a lot of people to pull it off. Since there is no way I can thank them all, I'll touch upon only a few.

Very special thanks are due to Charlie White, who took this project under his wing in its infant stages and put us in contact with the artists. Next in line is the Random House crew; it was a unique pleasure to work with Tony Schulte, Bob Scudellari, Peter Mollman and Gary Fisketjon, whose enthusiasm and assistance were invaluable.

And finally, my heartfelt thanks go to the remarkable staff that put this project together. Our writer, Elyce Wakerman, slaved to meet, and met, ridiculous deadlines. The contributions of the design staff—Bob Zoell, Rick Probst and Scott Griffiths—are evident on every spread and in the overall look of the book. The help and support of Gerald Lavelle and Stephen Rosenberg have been invaluable. And most of all I want to thank my wife, Aileen Sander, not only for the love and understanding that have helped me survive this tempest but also for her keen, intuitive sense of judgment that has guided and sustained us all.

—**Richard H. Childers**

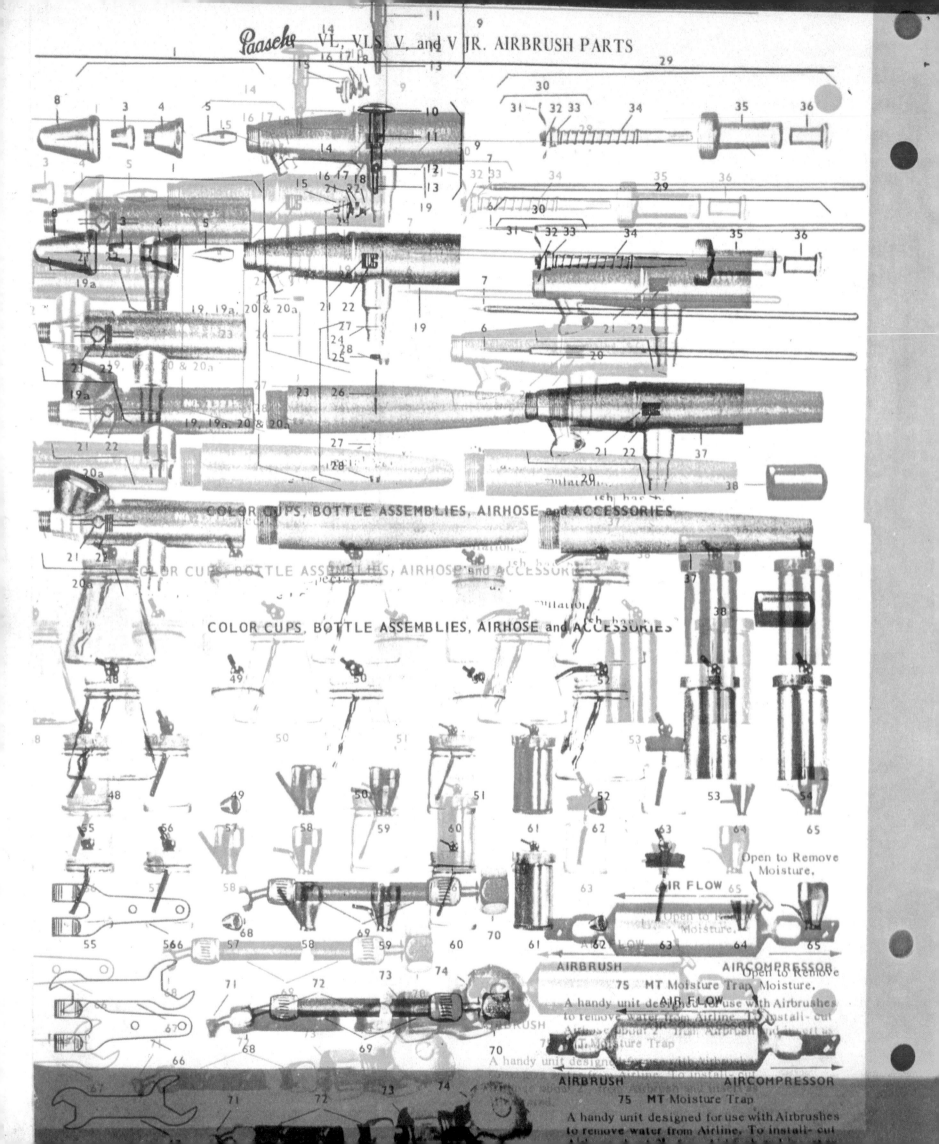

Paasche VL, VLS, V, and V JR. AIRBRUSH PARTS

COLOR CUPS, BOTTLE ASSEMBLIES, AIRHOSE and ACCESSORIES

Open to Remove Moisture.

AIR FLOW

AIRBRUSH   AIRCOMPRESSOR

75 MT Moisture Trap

A handy unit designed for use with Airbrushes to remove water from Airline. To install- cut Airhose about 2 ft. Airbrush end insert as